In Those Days

In Those Days

Collected Writings
on Arctic History

Book 5
Inuit and Explorers

by KENN HARPER

INHABIT
MEDIA

Published by Inhabit Media Inc.
www.inhabitmedia.com

Inhabit Media Inc. (Iqaluit) P.O. Box 11125, Iqaluit, Nunavut, X0A 1H0

Design and layout copyright © 2022 Inhabit Media Inc.
Text copyright © 2022 by Kenn Harper
Images copyright as indicated

Edited by Neil Christopher and Jessie Hale

Cover image: A portion of a photograph of a group of Inuit and sailors rescued from an ice floe in 1873. Source: Kenn Harper Collection.

This project was made possible in part by the Government of Canada.

We acknowledge the support of the Canada Council for the Arts for our publishing program.

Printed in Canada.

Library and Archives Canada Cataloguing in Publication

Title: Inuit and explorers / by Kenn Harper.
Names: Harper, Kenn, author.
Description: Series statement: In those days : collected writings on Arctic history ; book 5
Identifiers: Canadiana 20210370211 | ISBN 9781772274226 (softcover)
Subjects: LCSH: Inuit,—First contact with Europeans,—Canada, Northern. | LCSH: Inuit,—Canada, Northern,— History. | LCSH: Northwest Passage—Discovery and exploration. | LCSH: Northwest Passage—History.
 | LCSH: Canada, Northern—Discovery and exploration. | LCSH: Canada, Northern—History.
Classification: LCC E99.E7 H37 2022 | DDC 971.9004/9712—dc23

Table of Contents

Collected Writings

Introduction

This is the fifth volume to result from a series of articles that I wrote over a decade and a half under the title Taissumani for the Northern newspaper *Nunatsiaq News*. This volume presents stories of the interactions between Inuit and explorers, primarily in the Canadian Arctic but with a few digressions to Alaska, Greenland, and even Siberia. They are stories about culture contact—about interactions between two very different cultures. They tell of conflict and sometimes cooperation, about mutual confusions and sometimes understandings, about betrayal and loyalty. In researching some selections, I found an extensive paper trail; for others it is scanty. Inuit maintain some of these stories as part of their vibrant oral histories. We need to know these stories for a better understanding of the North today, and the events that made it what it is. They enhance our understanding of Northern people and contribute to our evolving appreciation of our shared history.

In Those Days

I lived in the Arctic for fifty years. My career has been varied; I've been a teacher, businessman, and consultant. I moved to the Arctic as a young man and worked for many years in small communities in the Qikiqtaaluk (then Baffin) region—one village where I lived had a population of only thirty-four. I also lived for two years in Qaanaaq, a community of five hundred in the remotest part of northern Greenland. Wherever I went, and whatever the job, I immersed myself in Inuktitut, the language of the Inuit.

In those wonderful days before television became a staple of Northern life, I visited the elders of the communities. I listened to their stories, drank tea and talked with them, and heard their perspectives on a way of life that was quickly passing.

I was also a voracious reader on all subjects Northern, and learned the standard histories of the Arctic from the usual sources. But I also sought out the lesser-known books and articles that informed me about Northern people and their experiences. In the process I became an avid book collector and writer.

All the stories collected in this volume originally appeared in my column, Taissumani, in *Nunatsiaq News*. *Taissumani* means "long ago." In colloquial English it might be glossed as "in those days," which is the title of this series. The columns appeared online as well as in the print edition of the paper. Because of this, it came as a surprise to me to learn that I had an international readership. I know this because of the comments that readers have sent me. I say it was a surprise because I initially thought of the columns as being stories for Northerners. No one was writing popular history for a Northern audience, be it Indigenous or non-Indigenous, and so I had decided that I would write stories that would appeal to, and inform, Northern people. Because of where I have lived and learned, and my knowledge of Inuktitut, these stories would usually (but not always) be about the Inuit North. The fact that readers elsewhere in the world show an interest in my stories is not only personally gratifying to me, but should be satisfying to Northerners as well—the world is interested in the Arctic.

I began writing the series in January of 2005, and ended it temporarily in 2015. I began it again three years later. I write about events, people, or places that relate to Arctic history. Most of the stories—for that is what they are, and I am simply a story-teller—deal with northern Canada, but some are set elsewhere. My definition of the Arctic is loose—it covers the areas where Inuit live, and so includes the sub-Arctic. Sometimes I stray a little even from those boundaries. I don't like restrictions, and *Nunatsiaq News* has given me free rein to write about what I think will interest its readers.

The stories are presented here substantially as they originally appeared in Taissumani, with the following cautions. Some stories that were originally presented in two or more parts have been presented here as single stories. A few stories are amalgamations from a number of columns. For most, the titles have changed. There have been minimal changes and occasional corrections to text. I have occasionally changed punctuation in direct quotations, if changing it to a more modern and expected style results in greater clarity. Similarly, I have sometimes regularized the spelling of personal and place names in quoted text.

The chapters have been organized in more or less chronological order. They are meant to be read independently.

Qujannamiik.
Kenn Harper
Ottawa, Canada

A Note on Word Choice

Inuk is a singular noun. It means, in a general sense, a person. In a specific sense, it also means one person of the group we know as Inuit, the people referred to historically as Eskimos. The plural form is *Inuit*.

A convention, which I follow, is that Inuit is the adjectival form, whether the modified noun is singular or plural; thus, an Inuit house, Inuit customs, an Inuit man, Inuit hunters.

The language spoken by Inuit in Canada is generically referred to as Inuktitut. In Nunavut in recent years the overall term for the language has become Inuktut, with Inuktitut being used to designate the dialects of the eastern and east-central Arctic, and Inuinnaqtun used to describe the dialect spoken in the western Kitikmeot Region. That spoken in Nunavik (northern Quebec) is still called Inuktitut. That spoken in Labrador is also called Inuktut. Greenlanders call their language Kalaallisut, but the Inughuit of northwestern Greenland refer to their speech as Inuktun.

The word *Eskimo* is not generally used today in Canada, although it is commonly used in Alaska. I use it if it is appropriate to do so in a historical context, and also in direct quotations. In these contexts, I also use the old (originally French) terms *Esquimau* (singular) and *Esquimaux* (plural).

I have generally used the historical spellings of Inuit personal names, sometimes because it is unclear what they were meant to be in the confusing idiosyncratic spellings of the time. The few exceptions are those where it is clear what an original spelling was meant to convey, or where there are a large number of variant spellings. For Inuit words other than names, I use the standard orthography ratified by the Inuit Language Commission in 1976.

Preface

The Canadian Arctic (and sub-Arctic) is the homeland of the Indigenous people we now know as Inuit. To early *Qallunaat* (non-Inuit) visitors to these lands, they were Eskimos, or sometimes Esquimaux.

The newcomers often claimed that they were the discoverers of these lands because they were new to them. They made these claims without embarrassment, seemingly oblivious to the fact that the Inuit were already there and had a dependence on and an attachment to their lands.

But the arrogance was even greater than a simple failure to recognize a prior and continuing occupation. Many of the newcomers, in exploring their newfound domains, attempted to maintain their own methods of travel by land in what to them was a harsh, even hostile, environment. This often worked well in the all-too-brief summers, but for Qallunaat who wintered—purposely, or as a result of being "frozen in"—the results were often disastrous. The clothing of Britain's Royal Navy was no match for the naturally insulated caribou-skin clothing of the Inuit. Canvas tents were frigid and damp compared with Inuit-constructed snow houses—the famous "igloos" of school geography texts—which were snug and cozy and impervious to the winds that often raged outside. And Inuit methods of travel over snow and ice, using teams of dogs attached by a fan hitch to sleds made of driftwood or, when wood was scarce, even large fish frozen together, were far superior to the man-hauled sleds that European and American visitors clung to for far too long.

Inevitably, some of the explorers learned from the local Inuit. Those who did were the most successful in their varied quests, as well as being the ones who survived.

Exploration was not just the quest for new land but often the search for new knowledge, sometimes about science but sometimes about previous expeditions which had come to grief.

John Franklin's first foray into what was to become the Canadian Arctic, accompanied by Dr. John Richardson and George Back—who would both go on to establish reputations of their own—was a land expedition to explore the north coast of the continent and add to our geographic knowledge. On this and a subsequent land expedition, he had the good sense to engage Inuit interpreters from Hudson Bay to assist him in his interactions with Inuit he would encounter, who, he anticipated, might never have seen white men before. He did not demonstrate the same good judgment on his final expedition in search of a Northwest Passage, a voyage that cost him his life and the lives of over one hundred men; one wonders if the outcome would have been different if he had been accompanied by one or more Inuit assistants.

An Inuk who was recruited for a Northern expedition was usually referred to as an interpreter. In fact, this was often a catch-all term applied to an Indigenous person who would fill the role of guide, hunter (if a man), seamstress (if a woman), and jack-of-all-trades. In fact, some possessed only rudimentary facility in the use of the English language. Ipiirvik (Ebierbing), often known as "Eskimo Joe," accompanied a number of Arctic expeditions. A chronicler of one of them noted, perhaps tongue-in-cheek, that "his accomplishments proved to be somewhat limited; for although to all appearance a master of the Eskimo tongue, and speaking its various dialects more or less fluently, he knows scarcely any English. This somewhat impairs his usefulness as interpreter."

Over time, explorers became more prepared for the realities of Northern conditions, often through their engagement with Inuit interpreters and guides, and their adoption of Inuit diet and travel techniques. Charles Francis Hall, for example, was not in search of new lands, but rather had a single-minded focus on learning the truth about Franklin's fate and finding any survivors; to do so he used Inuit methods of travel and relied heavily on the above-mentioned Ipiirvik and his wife, Tookoolito.

Sadly, the names of Inuit who interacted with explorers were often not recorded at all. They are simply "the Eskimos" or sometimes "my faithful Eskimos." Martin Frobisher's interaction with Inuit was so early that the term *Eskimo* had yet to be applied to them; he referred to them as a group as "the countrie people." He recorded the names of the three captives he took away to England in 1577, although in a quite garbled form. It remained

In Those Days

for Hall, through diligent questioning almost three hundred years later, to recover the name of one man who assisted Frobisher's abandoned sailors.

Hall, indeed, was intensely interested in the Inuit he met, and recorded in his notebooks much more than just the knowledge he sought about the Franklin expeditions. His work has proved indispensable to modern-day ethnographers who have the patience to decipher his cramped handwriting. It is worth mentioning that he, among only a few explorers, used the word *Inuit* in preference to *Eskimo* when describing the people.

Many explorers gave little or no acknowledgement to their Inuit assistants. Franklin's reports contain few references to his interpreters Hiutiruq (Junius) and Tatannuaq (Augustus) on his first expedition, or to Ouligbuck on his second. His contemporaries, William Edward Parry and George Lyon, were more generous; their narratives are replete with the names of Inuit they encountered in the Iglulik area, with anecdotes about many of them.

John Rae was a remarkable explorer, an expert Arctic traveller, and a man who respected Inuit and their abilities. From his writings, a picture emerges of two Inuit, the unfortunate Albert One-Eye, the only man Rae ever lost on an expedition, and the complicated William Ouligbuck. Similarly, Hall's long friendship with Tookoolito and Ipiirvik, who were with him on all three of his Arctic expeditions, allows detailed biographies to be constructed for both.

This book is not a history of Arctic exploration, or even of the Inuit role in Northern expeditions. It is not meant to be a comprehensive overview. Instead it is a compilation of previously published chapters of the story of Northern exploration, collected and edited here. Some explorers important to the history of Northern exploration are not included. Similarly, some Inuit who interacted meaningfully with explorers are not found in these pages. My goal was to select stories from my corpus of published articles on Northern exploration that bring the roles of the Inuit participants to the foreground. Nonetheless, the reader must keep in mind that the expeditions of which I write were not Inuit-centred or Inuit-led; they were Qallunaat expeditions in which Inuit played important parts.

To the extent that the expeditions described were successful, Inuit often contributed to those successes. This book attempts to give those Inuit their due.

Abduction

The "Countrie People" of Baffin Island Meet Martin Frobisher

The white man had never seen a kayak before. From an island in a large bay on the southeastern shores of Baffin Island, he surveyed the body of water that stretched out in front of him. This must surely be a passage to the west, he thought—a northwest passage.

Then he spotted objects in the water at a distance. An account written at the time explained, "And being ashore, upon the toppe of a hill, he perceived a number of small things fleeting in the Sea a farre off, whyche he supposed to be Porposes or Ceales, or some kinde of strange fishe: but coming nearer, he discovered them to be men, in small boates made of leather."

The year was 1576. The man was Martin Frobisher, a seaman and adventurer from England sent out by the Muscovy Company to find a passage through or around the North American continent to the riches of Asia.

When the men in small boats—Inuit—were seen, Frobisher and his captain, Christopher Hall, returned quickly to their ship, the *Gabriel*. They had no way of knowing whether the strangers would be friend or foe. Nor did they know what race of people they were. The word *Eskimo* doesn't appear in contemporary accounts of Frobisher's voyages—it didn't come into use until the 1600s. The Frobisher accounts simply call Inuit the "countrie people." Hall described them as resembling "Tartars [Asians], with long blacke haire, broad faces, and flatte noses, and tawnie in colour, wearing Seale skinnes." To add to Frobisher's unease, the English thought the Inuit were cannibals; George Best, who travelled on Frobisher's second Arctic voyage, wrote, "our flesh is so sweet meate for them, that they will hardly part from so good morsels."

Christopher Hall was the first to make actual contact with the Inuit. He went ashore in the *Gabriel*'s boat, a white flag waving to show his peaceful intent. Through signs, he invited an Inuk to accompany him back to the ship and left a member of his crew ashore as a hostage, to show his good faith. In effect, each side had a hostage. The Englishmen fed the Inuk aboard the ship—he found the food distasteful—and gave him wine; when the man returned to shore he told his fellows that he had been well treated. The English hostage returned to the ship. This first contact had been peaceful.

A large group of Inuit then approached the ship and boarded. They traded sealskin garments and raw meat and fish for English bells, looking glasses, and other baubles. They showed no fear of the Qallunaat. In fact, the Englishmen, who knew that no other voyages to this Northern land had been documented, nonetheless felt that the Inuit had seen white men before and were accustomed to trade. Dionysius Settle wrote, "It seemeth they have bene used to this trade, or traffique, with some other people adjoining, or not farre distant from their Countrey." Who might these unknown traders have been? The record is silent.

Frobisher himself went ashore to the Inuit settlement. One man returned to the ship with him, apparently having agreed—or so the Englishmen thought—to guide the ship through the "strait" to the west. But there was likely misunderstanding of the arrangement on both sides; on this first encounter, no party on either side had any idea of the language spoken by the other. Again, it is to Christopher Hall that we must turn for reports of the encounters—Frobisher himself could not write. Hall noted of the Inuit, "They spake, but we understood them not."

Five of Frobisher's men took the Inuk ashore in the ship's boats to get his kayak. But instead of putting him on land in sight of the ship, they rowed around a headland, where three of the Qallunaat went ashore with him. The boat, with two men in it, reappeared, and Frobisher made signs that they should return to the ship. But the boat disappeared again behind the headland, presumably to pick up the other men. The five men were never seen by Englishmen again.

Frobisher was distraught. He could ill afford to lose five men—leaving him with only thirteen—and the ship's boat. Nor was he pleased about the loss of the guide he thought he had hired. He waited at anchor for the night, then proceeded farther up the bay in the hope of finding other Inuit who had no knowledge

14

of what had transpired, so that he could seize some of them and hold them hostage for his missing men. But he encountered no more Inuit, and returned a few days later to the site of his men's disappearance.

Then a number of men in kayaks appeared. Frobisher prepared for a skirmish. But instead, the man who had been the first to board the ship some days earlier approached the vessel in a cautious but friendly manner, no doubt hoping to trade. Frobisher lured him close to the ship with a bell, which he dropped into the sea when the man reached for it. Then Frobisher lured him closer by ringing a larger bell over the side of the ship. As the Inuk reached for the bell, Frobisher seized the man's hand, then grasped his wrist with his other hand and lifted the man and his kayak out of the water and onto the deck of the ship in one smooth motion. A chronicler of Frobisher's voyage wrote that the unfortunate man "whereupon when he found himself in captivity . . . he bit his tongue in twain within his mouth."

Frobisher held the man for two days, hoping yet to exchange him for his five missing men and his much-needed boat. But the Inuit who came near the ship in their kayaks did not offer up the five men. Reconciling himself to his losses, and unable to repair his strained relationship with the Inuit, Frobisher gave up his mission. On August 25, with the unfortunate Inuk still onboard, he set sail for England.

The hostage was now a captive and could at least be used to prove to Queen Elizabeth I that Frobisher had reached a far-off land.

They reached London on October 9, where the Inuk—whose name was never recorded—became the talk of the town. George Best described him as "this strange infidel, whose like was never seen, read, nor heard of before, and whose language was neither known nor understood of any." Michael Lok, Frobisher's principal financial backer, said he was "a wonder unto the whole city," and described his countenance as "sullen or churlish and sharp withal."

Misunderstandings resulting from language differences remained a problem. In England, the Inuit captive told John Dee, the court astronomer and adviser to the queen, that his land was called Pyckenay. As the later explorer Vilhjalmur Stefansson pointed out, "When asked where something is, Eskimos may well reply, pikani which, while it literally means 'up there', is understood to mean 'up on the high land'. This the English might well mistake for the name of a district." Similarly, the Inuk told Dee that he had been willing to guide Frobisher to "Mania"; Dee took this to mean the mythical Straits of Anian, a part of the equally mythical Northwest Passage. Stefansson pointed out, however, that when the man was being questioned, there was likely a map before him "and that the Eskimo, putting his finger on a district farther west than Frobisher Bay, used the expression mani [*maani*], meaning 'here'."

Unfortunately the captive did not survive long. He died in London and was buried in the Church of St. Olave, a church that still stands near the Tower of London. The church records, however, do not record his burial, and so he remains nameless, the first recorded casualty in a clash of cultures in the Canadian Arctic.

* * *

What happened to Frobisher's five missing men over four centuries ago? They were last seen by their fellow Qallunaat on August 20, 1576. The British sailors aboard the *Gabriel* assumed that they had been captured, held against their will, and probably murdered. But over two centuries later, Inuit oral history told a different tale.

The following year, Frobisher returned to Cyrus Field Bay at the mouth of the larger bay that bears his name in southeastern Baffin Island, this time with three ships. He was, once again, searching for the Northwest Passage, but he also hoped to mine gold. Of course, he was most curious about the fate of his five men, and held out hope that they were still alive.

On this expedition, relations with the Inuit were no better than the previous year. Battles were held, and a number of Inuit were killed. In one skirmish, Frobisher himself was famously shot in the buttock with an arrow.

Just as on the previous expedition, so now Frobisher took one of the "countrie people," a man, as captive. He showed him pictures of the Inuk taken captive to England the previous year. The man was astonished. Thinking the depiction was a living, though miniaturized, human being, he spoke to it and was disappointed when he received no response. The Inuk "with great noise and cries, ceased not wondering, thinking that we could make men live or die at our pleasure."

With his captive in tow, Frobisher landed on Countess of Warwick Island (now called Kodlunarn Island—White Man's Island), determined to learn the fate of his men. His miners, meanwhile, began excavating there.

At one point, the captive arranged five sticks in a circle with a small bone in the middle. The Englishmen at first thought this was "some charm or witchcraft," but finally concluded that it was meant as a sign to his fellow Inuit that he, represented by the bone, had been taken prisoner as retribution for the five men the Inuit had presumably seized the previous year.

In Those Days

Captain Yorke of the vessel *Michael* found Qallunaat cloth-ing—"sundry articles of the apparel"—and mismatched shoes in a tent on the southwestern shore of the sound. Thinking that the five men might still be alive, he left a note; in the parlance of the time, he "left his mind behind him in writing, with pen, ink, and paper also, whereby our poor captive countrymen . . . might know their friends' minds . . . and likewise return their answer."

By signs, one group of Inuit communicated that three of the men were still alive, and that Frobisher should send a letter to them—some of them had seen Frobisher and his men writing in journals and logs aboard ship and had concluded that this was some means of communication. Frobisher wrote a letter and sent writing supplies with the Inuit so that the captive men might reply. But no answer was ever received. In his letter, Frobisher assured his missing men "that if they deliver you not, I will not leave a man alive in their country."

Frobisher's efforts to find his missing men—indeed, even to learn if they were dead or alive—were in vain. Relations with the Inuit deteriorated. A vicious battle took place at a locale after-wards called Bloody Point, where a number of Inuit were killed and a woman and her child taken prisoner. When Frobisher left for England, it was with three captives: the man, whose name has been recorded as Calichoe or Callichogh; the woman called Egnoge or Ignorth, which was simply a sailor's attempt to say *Arnaq* (woman); and the child, Nutioc, probably *Nutaraq* (child).

* * *

In 1860 Charles Francis Hall, a printer and journalist from Cincinnati, hitched a ride to the Arctic on a whaling ship, the

George Henry. He had become obsessed with the fate of the missing British expedition commanded by Sir John Franklin, which had set off in search of a Northwest Passage in 1845 and never returned. Despite the discovery of numerous bodies of men who had perished in that expedition in the central Arctic, Hall believed that some men, perhaps led by Captain Crozier, a man who had previously wintered successfully in the Arctic, had survived. His task was to find them.

But the *George Henry* was bound for Cyrus Field Bay, hundreds of miles from where Franklin was presumed to have perished. Hall hoped to recruit Inuit and travel from there to King William Island in his fanatical quest for survivors of the lost expedition. When he realized he had no hope of carrying out his plan, he made the best of it and devoted his time to learning Inuit ways and survival skills, the better to prepare himself for a later trip to the central Arctic. Instead of learning the fate of Franklin, Hall unexpectedly uncovered the story of Frobisher's three expeditions to the area, preserved for almost three hundred years in the memories of Inuit.

While exploring Frobisher Bay, Hall met the oldest woman in the area, Uqijjuaqsi Nanuq—he spelled her name Ookijoxy Ninoo—and learned from her that

> five white men were captured by Innuit people at the time of the appearance of the ships a great many years ago; that these men wintered on shore (whether one, two, three, or more winters, could not say); that they lived among the Innuits; that they afterward built an oomien [*umiaq*] (large boat), and put a mast into her, and had sails; that early in the season . . . they endeavoured to depart; that, in the effort,

In Those Days

some froze their hands; but that finally they succeeded in getting into open water, and away they went, which was the last seen or heard of them.[1]

Through Hall's interpreter Tookoolito, the old woman later added details, some slightly contradictory, to her account.

The white men had apparently gotten along well with the Inuit, and especially with one man, whose name was Eloudjuarng. He was, Hall wrote, "a great man or chief among the Inuit." Tookoolito said he was "All same as king." When the white men were about to set out for home, Eloudjuarng composed a song wishing them a quick and safe passage, "and he caused his people, who were very numerous, to sing it." But the white men failed in their attempt to flee the country, and, in this version of the story, "finally froze to death."

On Kodlunarn Island, Hall discovered a "ship's trench." Inuit told him that this was where the "small ship" was constructed. The Qallunaat took the boat to nearby Tikkoon Point, where they installed a mast at the bluff called Nepouetiesupbing—a place "to set up a mast." Finding the ship's trench seemed to verify, for Hall, the story told by Uqijjuaqsi about the events of so long ago.

That would seem to solve the mystery of what happened to the five missing men. But does it? Archaeologist Susan Rowley, in her research into this story, noted, "It is impossible to put together a story of the qallunaat who built the ship on Kodlunarn by simply adding all the information together. Some of the testimony is contradictory, while some comes from people who are less well informed than others." Indeed, the story has some rather large holes in it.

---

[1] Charles Francis Hall, *Life with the Esquimaux* (London: Sampson, Low, Son, and Marston, 1864), 303.

Why would the five missing men have spent the winter of 1576–77 on Kodlunarn Island—an island that Frobisher had not "discovered" in 1576?

If they had, why did Frobisher not find any trace of them there when he did explore the island in 1577?

Why did Frobisher not report a "ship's trench" on the island in that year?

What materials would the five missing men have used to build a boat there? The voyage of 1576 had left no spare materials anywhere in the vicinity. Their departure is said to have happened early in the following season, before much water appeared. Given the harshness and length of the winter, even had there been materials, there would have been precious little time for five men (or three, if one Inuit report was correct) to build a "small ship." For answers to these questions, we must look at the events of the following year.

Frobisher made a third voyage to the same area in 1578. Uqijjuaqsi told Hall that he came with "am-a-su-ad-lo oo-moo-arch-chu-a [*amisualuk umiarjuat*]"—"a great many ships." She was right: he had arrived with a fleet of fifteen vessels, the largest convoy to visit the Arctic until modern times. Before the conclusion of that season's activities, Frobisher constructed a stone house on Kodlunarn Island and stashed lumber, iron, and other goods there, anticipating that he would return yet again the following year.

Arctic archaeologist William Fitzhugh has noted that the ships departed the area that year in chaos during a fierce storm. Accounts of the hectic departure are murky, but a number of the ships' boats and men were lost. A pinnace sent from the *Gabriel* to catch up with the *Moone* probably did not reach the latter ship.

In Those Days

It could, of course, have been lost with all its men. But it may have survived the storm and, when the men realized that all the ships had departed, returned to the house on Kodlunarn Island. There its crew—which would have numbered considerably more than five—may have excavated what became known as the "ship's trench," or modified one of Frobisher's "mines" into such a trench.

They may have had the time and the skills to use the materials left on the island to build themselves a boat, install a mast, and attempt to sail home. Living peacefully among the Inuit, they may not even have started construction during the first year, until they realized that no more ships were coming to Frobisher Bay.

But what of Uqijjuaqsi's tale? It was a remarkable story, well preserved for nine generations, by Hall's reckoning. Her two tellings of it are not without inconsistencies. But oral histories, especially recollections of events that happened a very long time ago, often suffer from conflation, defined by Susan Rowley as "the collation of two events, sometimes separated in time, into one." This is probably what happened with the oral histories recounted by Uqijjuaqsi. In this scenario, the refugees from the *Gabriel*'s pinnace lost in 1578 were eventually replaced in memory by the five originally missing men. That's why Frobisher found no trace of those first men on Kodlunarn Island in 1577.

This explanation, which involved friendly relations between Inuit and the crew of the pinnace on Kodlunarn Island, explains the construction of the escape boat there, and the fate of the men from the pinnace. But what of the five missing men from 1576? It leaves their fate still unspoken.

Robert McGhee, an Arctic archaeologist and historian, in considering the events of 1576, felt that the Inuit may well have

wanted to steal the ship's boat, wood being a very valuable com-
modity, but that they would have no other reason to hold the men
hostage. He suggests, then, that the Englishmen could have acted
voluntarily. He speculated: "An invitation to come ashore and further their acquaintance, as well as to walk freely on the dry tundra
and drink clean water from a stream, may have been too entic-
ing to resist." According to this scenario, they may have deserted.
Their long-term fate, McGhee wrote, "would have been entirely
dependent on the nature of the camp leader."

There is a strange footnote to this story. In 1862 Hall learned of
an unusual monument said to have been erected by the Qallunaat
from Frobisher's ships in Newton's (now Newton) Fiord and
revered by Inuit. Uqijjuaqsi is once again the source of the story:
"The monument itself is not on very high land. The Innuits for
a very long time, and down even to the present day, have been
in the habit of going there; and wishing success in hunting, they
would give it presents of young tuktoo [caribou] meat, bows and
arrows, beads, &c. hanging the same on it or placing them close
about it. It was on all occasions treated with great respect, the
belief being that he who gave much to the monument would
kill much game." The old lady concluded: "This stone marker of
Kod-lu-nars great help to Innuits—Always makes tuktoo plenty
there. Every Innuit knows all about this." In the old lady's sketch
of herself "performing her devotions" to the monument, it does
not appear to be a traditional cairn. Was this strange monument
erected by Frobisher's ship's crew, or later by the five missing men
or the pinnace crew?

"They Spake, But We Understood Them Not"

Christopher Hall's Inuktitut Word List

In 1576, on Martin Frobisher's first voyage, Christopher Hall or one of his seamen collected a list of seventeen Inuktitut words.

The list is the earliest Inuit vocabulary collected by Europeans.

One must remember that Europeans had no knowledge of Inuit at this time, and that the sailor who collected the wordlist, as interested as he might have been in the new people he had just met, was undoubtedly a monolingual speaker of English. He would have equated the sounds he heard from the Inuit with sounds with which he was familiar in his own language, and written them clumsily in an orthography based on the English of his time.

He would have pointed to objects or touched them and asked what they were. Thus, the wordlist is naturally top-heavy with nouns and deficient in verbs.

He would have been unaware that the Inuit language, unlike English, is a highly inflected language, and he would therefore not have recognized endings on words and would have assumed the naming feature of the word or utterance to be everything he heard, including any ending.

Indeed, he would not have known what constituted a word. He would have been unaware of what, to people familiar with Inuktitut, is an old adage—that in Inuktitut a word can be a sentence. This describes in simple terms the structure of Inuktitut in which a sentence—or an utterance—can be built up by adding numerous suffixes to a base word.

Given the differences between the uninflected English language of our sailor and the highly inflected and unrelated language of his mysterious Inuit informants, the miracle is that we can decipher any of the words on the list. In fact, we can decipher all but one, and at the same time learn something of the structure of the Inuit language of southern Baffin in the late sixteenth century.

The list collected was appended to Christopher Hall's account of Frobisher's first voyage, under the title "The language of the people of Meta incognita." It is as follows:

In Those Days

Argoteyt, a hand
Cangnawe, a nose
Arered, an eye
Keiotot, a tooth
Mutchater, the head
Chewat, an eare
Comagaye, a legge
Atoniagay, a foote
Callagay, a paire of breeches
Attegay, a coate
Polleuetagay, a knife
Accaskay, a shippe
Coblone, a thumbe
Teckkere, the foremost finger
Ketteckle, the middle finger
Mekellacane, the fourth finger
Yacketrone, the little finger[2]

The first scholar to comment, although briefly, on this word-list was the Alaskan missionary Francis Barnum in his "Grammatical Fundamentals of the Innuit Language as spoken by the Eskimo of the Western Coast of Alaska." Unfortunately, as the title indicates, Barnum had no direct experience of eastern Canadian dialects and restricted his comments on the list to the following: "Some of these words are interesting from the fact that they show the difficulty of the first attempt at obtaining a vocabulary, owing to not knowing the grammatical

---

[2] Adapted from "Appendix 7. The Eskimo Words in Frobisher's Voyages," in Vilhjalmur Stefansson (ed.), *The Three Voyages of Martin Frobisher. Volume 2* (London: The Argonaut Press, 1938), 233–236.

structure of the language, and to the mistakes arising from mutual miscomprehension."

The list has been analyzed in detail by a number of Northern and linguistic scholars, among them Danish philologist William Thalbitzer, the explorer Vilhjalmur Stefansson, and Canadian linguist Louis-Jacques Dorais.

Let's consider first the words about which there can be no doubt as to meaning. The stems of these words, and in some cases the entire words, are easily recognizable as modern Inuit words. I will not dwell on the endings that have been appended. In some cases they are a second-person singular adjectival ending, as one would expect if the sailor pointed to something of his and asked what it was—for example, your hands, your nose.

The easily recognizable words are:

Argoteyt, a hand	*aggaak*: hands
Cangnawe, a nose	*qingaq*: nose
Keiotot, a tooth	*kigutit*: tooth
Chewat, an eare	*suit*: ear
Callagay, a paire of breeches	*qarliik*: pants, or qarligiik: pants
Attegay, a coat	*atigi*: inner parka
Coblone, a thumbe	*kublu*: thumb
Teckkere, the foremost finger	*tikiq*: index finger
Ketteckle, the middle finger	*qitiqłiq*: middle finger
Mekellacane, the fourth finger	*mikiliraq*: third finger (ring finger)

One of these may be ambiguous. Thalbitzer noted that cangnawe may be from either *qingaq* ("nose"), or *qaniq* ("mouth"). Indeed the sound seems closer to the word for mouth than to nose. One can imagine a situation in which the sailor was pointing to, rather than touching, the object and some confusion arose.

> The words left to decipher are these:
> Arered, an eye
> Mutchater, the head
> Comagaye, a legge
> Atoniagay, a foote
> Polleuetagay, a knife
> Accaskay, a shippe
> Yacketrone, the little finger

Four of these are relatively easy.

Mutchater, given in the list as "the head," is more readily intelligible when the initial consonant is changed to "n" and when the final consonant is changed to "t." The word can then be seen to be nutchatet. In modern Inuktitut, this word is *nujatit*—"your hair." The sailor interpreted this as being the word for "head" rather than "hair."

Thalbitzer in his analysis provides linguistic reasons why arered can be equated with isit—"your eye"—in today's language, *ijiit*.

Similarly, he equates yacketrone with the Greenlandic *eqerqune*—"on your little finger." In modern Canadian Inuktitut this would be *iqiqquni*, from the word for little finger—*iqiqquq*.

The word polleuetagay is from *pilaut* or *pilauti*, meaning a knife. That leaves three:

Comagaye, a legge
Atoniagay, a foote
Accaskay, a shippe

Stefansson has suggested that comagaye is derived from *kamik*—
"boot." Dorais has further suggested kamegik—"a pair of boots."
One can imagine the sailor pointing to the lower leg, covered
with a high boot, and assuming the word given to mean leg rather
than boot.

Thalbitzer has also suggested that atoniagay is derived from a
word he gives in Greenlandic spelling as atorniagai—"the one he
uses." Again, Stefansson has found this implausible and suggested
that the word comes from atungaq—"boot sole." But Thalbitzer's
explanation, slightly modified, makes more sense. Imagine that
the sailor, rather than wearing the boot while eliciting the term,
is, instead, holding it. Perhaps motioning to signify his intention
to put it on, he asks his Inuit informant its name. The informant
may have given him a word—*aturniagait*—meaning "that which
you are going to use" or "that which you are going to put on."

This leaves one word: accaskay—"a ship." Thalbitzer is silent
on this word. Stefansson and Dorais each made suggestions, both
implausible. Indeed Stefansson calls his own suggestion "mere
speculation" and notes, "One might say almost anything while
looking at a ship." The word remains a mystery.

"Take Heed of the Savage People"

Hudson's Mutineers Meet the Inuit

I n the summer of 1611, a mutiny occurred on Henry Hudson's ship the *Discovery*. Having spent a difficult winter in James Bay, members of the crew were concerned about Hudson's secrecy and his seeming desire to loiter there, searching every bay and river estuary that might lead to a passage to the Pacific. The conspirators cast Hudson, his son John, and seven other men, including those who were sick, adrift in a tiny shallop. The *Discovery* then began its tortuous return to

England under the leadership of Henry Greene and Robert Juet.

On July 26 the ship reached Cape Wolstenholme, the north-westernmost tip of present-day Nunavik (the Inuit area of northern Quebec), where the crew would naturally expect to make a right turn into Hudson Strait. But first there was the matter of food. Their supplies were almost exhausted. In their haste, they had ignored the rich sea mammal resources of Hudson Bay's east coast. So a detour was made to East Digges Island, where the men knew there was a murre colony. For some of this motley crew, it was a fatal detour.

A shore party of Englishmen encountered a group of Inuit camped on the island, there for the same purpose, to secure a supply of seabirds as food. The two groups made contact. Although there is no record of previous contact between white men and Inuit in this area, the Inuit probably knew about the existence of strangers like these from across the sea. Inuit on Baffin Island had encountered Qallunaat on the earlier Frobisher expeditions, and those on the Labrador coast had periodic contact with Basque, French, and English fishermen. News of these strangers and their trade goods would have reached Nunavik from one or both of these sources.

The Inuit showed the white men their way of knocking the murres from the cliffs with long poles. The white men demonstrated their method—blasting them out of the air, seven or eight at a time, with a musket shot.

After the visit to the bird cliffs, the two groups got down to the business of trade. The Inuit offered many products of the land and sea, but the English were interested only in walrus ivory. They got what they wanted in return for a knife and two glass buttons. By signs, the Inuit told Henry Greene that his party should return the next day to barter for fresh meat. Or so Greene thought.

31

In Those Days

The following day Greene returned with five men in the ship's boat. They saw the Inuit "dancing and leaping" on the hills as they put in to a sheltered cove. The Inuit rushed forward, anxious to barter. Greene and another man showed off their trade items: bells, mirrors, and a Jew's harp. One man clamoured into the ship's boat where Habakkuk Prickett sat. Prickett, nervous, motioned for him to go ashore. But another Inuk was already in the boat and attempted to stab Prickett. The Englishman fended off the main thrust of the strike but still sustained wounds to his arm, chest, and thigh. Finally he managed to overpower his assailant and stabbed him in the chest and throat.

Meanwhile other Inuit had attacked the Englishmen who were ashore. Two were virtually disembowelled. But all made it to the shallop and fled for the *Discovery*, which lay a short distance away. Next the Inuit used their bows and arrows, and shot Henry Greene dead. Another arrow struck Prickett in the back, but he survived. His Inuit attacker and the two men who had been most seriously wounded on shore all died aboard the *Discovery* that very day, another man two days later. Of the six men of the shore party, only Prickett and one other man survived.

From East Digges Island the survivors sailed the *Discovery* through Hudson Strait and across the Atlantic to England. Upon their arrival they had a lot of explaining to do. Mutiny was a serious offence, and the task of this malnourished group of adventurers was to present an alibi that would hold water, if they were to avoid possible death sentences.

One way they did this was to hold out the hope that their knowledge of the route to and through Hudson Bay held value for enterprising investors anxious to discover the Northwest Passage, and with it a route to the riches of the Orient.

Perhaps no one was more adept in this regard than the wily Habakkuk Prickett, who was super-cargo on the expedition. A super-cargo was essentially a passenger, not a part of a ship's working crew, put aboard as a representative of the investors or of the ship's owners. Prickett represented the interests of Sir Thomas Smythe of the Haberdasher's Company—and that is almost all we know of him.

Prickett's tack, in trying to convince the investors that they should back further expeditions to the northwest, despite having just backed one that achieved nothing, centred in part on the attack by the Inuit. More to the point, it centred on the knife that an Inuk had wielded against him with such force that it had come very close to rendering him a corpse. Samuel Purchas, an English cleric and publisher of travel narratives, acquired some of Prickett's papers and wrote in 1625 about his and his mates' experiences and the arguments for a passage through North America to the Pacific. Purchas wrote: "The weapons and arts which they [the mutineers] saw, beyond those of other savages, are arguments hereof. He which assaulted Prickett in the boat, had a weapon broad and sharp indented, of bright steel (such as they use in Java), riveted into a handle of morse [walrus] tooth."

The conclusion that Prickett had, then, tried to convey was that these Inuit had come from the Pacific, or that the knife had come from the Pacific and made its way eastward through the long-sought passage through trade.

Prickett had described a knife very un-Inuit in character. The event had happened in 1611; no ships were known to have traversed Hudson Strait by that date—George Weymouth's 1602 expedition had entered the strait, but only for a short distance. Where had this steel-bladed knife come from?

In Those Days

Of course, there is the possibility that Prickett fabricated his description of the weapon. But if he did not, and if the knife was as described, it had certainly not come from the Orient. Probably it had come from the southern reaches of the Labrador coast, where Inuit were known to trade with whalers and fishermen, and been traded from hand to hand up the coast. It might have come, too, from across Hudson Strait, from the Inuit of Baffin Island. George Best, who left an account of Martin Frobisher's earlier voyages to Frobisher Bay, wrote of the Inuit encountered there that "it appeereth they trade with other nations which dwell farre off." Many modern scholars also suspect that Basque whalers may have whaled as far north as Davis Strait, and with whaling generally came trade.

No one knows what happened to the knife that tore into Habakkuk Prickett's thigh. Prickett had overpowered the Inuk and took him aboard ship, where he died. Prickett may have kept the knife, although Samuel Purchas wrote about it only from Prickett's description. Perhaps it lies today, unidentified, in a museum or a damp British attic, an unknown relic of an attack, the motives for which are still a mystery.

It is an often-quoted cliché that the winners get to write history. However, the Inuit must be counted the winners in this inexplicable attack. But the losers wrote the account. Habakkuk Prickett's story is the only recounting we have of this bloody episode. He blamed it all on Henry Greene and suggested that "we take heed of the savage people." Whether the attack by the Inuit was unprovoked or the result of a tragic misunderstanding, we will never know.

Slaughter at Bloody Fall

The image is unforgettable: that of a dying young Inuit woman writhing in pain, her body pierced by spears, while grasping for the legs of a white explorer and begging him for assistance that never came. And yet the image is only in the mind of the reader, an image formed from the powerful verbal description left by the explorer Samuel Hearne. Surprisingly, his published narrative contains no such illustration. Yet that mental image captures one of the most iconic events in the history of the North. Popular historian Ken McGoogan calls it "one of the most controversial moments in Canadian history."

Winston Churchill once wrote, "History will be kind to me, because I intend to write it." Samuel Hearne got to write the history of this event, and there are no competing versions. As a result, history has generally been kind to Hearne. Generally, but not always.

In Those Days

The names of Samuel Hearne and a Chipewyan Indian man named Matonabbee are inextricably linked in Northern history. Their backgrounds could not have been more dissimilar, but despite that, they became friends.

Hearne was born in England in 1745. Orphaned at a young age, like many boys of the time, he entered the service of the Royal Navy at the age of eleven. In 1766 he joined the Hudson's Bay Company as mate on a company vessel that traded with the Inuit north of Prince of Wales Fort, built at Churchill in 1717. The following year he discovered the sad fate of James Knight and the men of an earlier company expedition when he found their remains on Marble Island.

The Hudson's Bay Company had long faced criticism for focusing its efforts on commercial coastal trade while neglecting the exploration of its inland territory and the search for a Northwest Passage. Knight's expedition, which had left England in 1719, had ambitiously aimed to remedy that—he would seek the legendary Strait of Anian, which was thought to lead to a Northwest Passage, expand trade, establish a whaling industry, and discover gold and copper mines reported by the Chipewyans. But Knight and his men were never again seen by white men; their ships wrecked on Marble Island, and they were all dead within two years.

Nonetheless, reports of a copper mine far to the west persisted. Moses Norton, the factor under whom Hearne served, became obsessed by persistent Chipewyan reports of the "far-away metal river." When they brought specimens of the ore to the fort in 1767, that only fuelled Norton's intention to find and exploit the deposits.

In November two years later, Norton dispatched Hearne, described as "diligent and trustworthy but not an assertive character," with two white servants and a party of Indians, prepared for a journey of up to two years. They were to head northwest and find the copper mines. But the attempt was a disaster, and Hearne was back at Prince of Wales Fort before Christmas. The following year he made another attempt, which was also unsuccessful. In September, though, while still making his way back to the post, he met the Indian leader Matonabbee, who was on his way to Churchill to trade. The two reached the post together on November 25. Hearne described the man as the "most sociable, kind and sensible Indian I had ever met with."

Matonabbee had been born about 1736 to a Chipewyan father and a mother described only as a "slave woman." Her origins are unknown; she may have been Cree. She had been a slave to an Indian who traded her to the Hudson's Bay Company at Churchill. Richard Norton, manager of the post, gave her to a Chipewyan man; Matonabbee was their son. Soon after, both parents were dead, and Richard Norton unofficially adopted the boy. But when Norton retired in 1741, Matonabbee, still a child, rejoined his Chipewyan relatives. Eleven years later, in his late teens, he returned to the post and was hired by the company as a hunter to supply game.

At Churchill, Matonabbee learned the Cree language and "made some progress in English," but felt that Christianity was "too deep and intricate for his comprehension." Hearne thought him punctual, truthful, and scrupulous, possessed of a "natural good sense and liberality of sentiment." Nearly six feet tall, he was strong, energetic, and courageous. The new manager at Churchill, Ferdinand Jacobs, selected Matonabbee to make peace between the Chipewyans and their long-standing rivals, the western Cree. Matonabbee worked patiently over many years to bring about peace and establish trade between the two groups. During this period he acquired influence and prestige as a middleman in the fur trade. He also acquired at least six wives.

Matonabbee had been to the alleged copper mines in the north-west and said that he had had friendly relations with the Inuit he encountered there, giving them "small presents of such articles as they [the Chipewyans] could best spare."

After Hearne's return from the aborted second journey in search of the copper mine, he spent only twelve days at the trading post before Norton again directed him to take up the search, this time in company with Matonabbee. Hearne's writings make it quite clear that Matonabbee was in charge. Hearne later wrote of him in endearing terms, describing his "benevolence and universal humanity to all the human race, according to his abilities." This is a remarkable characterization in light of Hearne's knowledge that Matonabbee had murdered one of his spouses for casting doubt on his ability to satisfy all his wives—Hearne, in an under-statement, admitted that the man was prone to jealousy, which sometimes took him "beyond the bounds of humanity." But the characterization is even more remarkable considering the events that happened when the party reached the Coppermine River.

The party travelled west during the winter, then turned north-ward in April. At Clowey Lake, Hearne was disillusioned when a large group of western Indians joined their party with the expressed intent of murdering any Inuit that they might encounter at the mouth of the Coppermine. Hearne protested, but to no avail, and eventually gave up, to the point that, amazingly, he wrote in his journal that "I did not care if they rendered the name and race of the Esquimaux extinct."

On July 17, 1771 Hearne's worst fears were realized when the party surprised a camp of Inuit sleeping in their tents near the mouth of the river. That morning Hearne's Indian guides killed over twenty Inuit—men, women, and children. Hearne left a heart-wrenching description of the slaughter:

> The shrieks and groans of the poor expiring wretches were truly dreadful; and my horror was much increased at seeing a young girl, seemingly about eighteen years of age, killed so near me, that when the first spear was stuck into her side she fell down at my feet and twisted round my legs, so that it was with difficulty that I could disengage myself from her dying gasps. As two Indian men pursued this unfortunate victim, I solicited very hard for her life; but the murderers made no reply till they had stuck both their spears through her body and transfixed her to the ground. They then looked me sternly in the face, and began to ridicule me, by asking if I wanted an Esquimaux wife; and paid not the smallest regard to the shrieks and agony of the poor wretch, who was twining round their spears like an eel![3]

Hearne was unable to prevent the massacre. Matonabbee made no attempt to stop the carnage and participated willingly in it. Hearne named the spot Bloody Fall, a name which eventually morphed into Bloody Falls. It is near present-day Kugluktuk. The name lives on in infamy today.

Samuel Hearne's original journals have not survived, but he eventually prepared a narrative of his trip to the Coppermine River for publication. It finally appeared in print in 1795, three years after his death and twenty-four years after the massacre. The book was

---

[3] Samuel Hearne, *A Journey from Prince of Wales's Fort in Hudson's Bay to the Northern Ocean* (London: A. Strahan and T. Cadell, 1795), 153–54.

an instant success. Reviewers pronounced Hearne to have been "a judicious observer" and "a candid and faithful reporter of facts." Of course, they seized on Hearne's relatively brief description of the massacre as the highlight of the lengthy book.

This is perhaps explained by placing the narrative in its time. The horrors of the French Revolution, with its attendant savagery, had affected European sensibilities, particularly in England, where the wealthy class feared a similar occurrence. As scholar Emilie Cameron has pointed out in her analysis of the Hearne tale, "stories about death, torture, violence, and mass murder gained unprecedented appeal in Britain during the 1790s." Hearne's account fit right in.

But is Hearne's report really what happened? Was he a "candid and faithful reporter"?

Some have suggested that Hearne's published work was shaped and reshaped by him over the years, then perhaps reshaped again by an editor after his death. Hearne himself wrote in his preface, "I have at my leisure hours recopied all my Journals into one book, and in some instances added to the remarks I had before made." In other words, he revised and edited. But to what purpose? Some of his changes may have been to assuage his own guilt at his participation in the massacre, if only as a spectator. Perhaps this section, immediately after he had painted the image of the young woman "twining round their spears like an eel," was one of those additions:

> Indeed, after receiving much abusive language from them [the Chipewyans] on the occasion, I was at length obliged to desire that they would be more expeditious in dispatching their victim out of her misery, otherwise I should be obliged, out of

pity, to assist in the friendly office of putting an end to the existence of a fellow-creature who was so cruelly wounded. On this request being made, one of the Indians hastily drew his spear from the place where it was first lodged, and pierced it through her breast near the heart. . . . My situation and the terror of my mind at beholding this butchery, cannot easily be conceived, much less described; though I summed up all the fortitude I was master of on the occasion, it was with difficulty that I could refrain from tears.[4]

Certainly this remark was added some time later: "even at this hour I cannot reflect on the transactions of that horrid day without shedding tears."

To what purpose were Hearne's words altered, either by himself or by a subsequent editor? Undoubtedly it was to turn field notes into a compelling and saleable manuscript, but also to heighten the action, especially of the scene of carnage, to entice a readership hungry for the exotic and the "savage." Scholar Bruce Greenfield, while posing an intriguing question in the title of an article on the subject, "Can Fur Traders Have Feelings?," rejected the suggestion of other critics that "the emotionality of Hearne's expression" was "superimposed by another hand," and credits Hearne with the authorship of his narrative. He concludes that Hearne was a literate, cultured man, and the horror and the sympathy were all his.

But there has been another, more serious question posed about Hearne's tale. Was he even there? Or did he simply compose the horrific scene from his own imagination and reports of the Chipewyans, perhaps even Matonabbee himself?

---

[4] Ibid., 154.

In Those Days

Fifty years to the day after the massacre at Bloody Fall, another British exploring party, that of John Franklin, was travelling down the Coppermine River. The following day they reached its mouth. John Richardson, the expedition's doctor, wrote that they had earlier met several old Indian men who had previously met Hearne and were knowledgeable about his journey:

> The leading facts of his journey are still current subjects of tradition among that tribe [Yellowknives Dene, then called the Copper Indians], as well as with the Northern Indians [Chipewyans]; and from all that we have been able to collect in the fur countries, as well as from an attentive examination of his narrative, we are led to conclude that he visited the various places marked in his map, in the order in which they stand; that all the rivers and lakes which he names actually exist; and that he has correctly described the general physical features of the country he traversed. His description of the lower part of the Coppermine River, in particular, is evidently of one who has been on the spot.[5]

But three pages later, Richardson states, "We are led to conclude that he did not actually go down to the sea, but was content to view it from the top of the hill which overhangs the falls."

Richardson's carefully chosen words are designed to avoid impugning the integrity of a former explorer apparently held in high regard. He avoids any mention of the massacre, and

---

[5] John Richardson, "Digression Concerning Hearne's Route," in George Back, *Narrative of the Arctic Land Expedition to the Mouth of the Great Fish River and Along the Shores of the Arctic Ocean, in the Years 1833, 1834, and 1835* (London: John Murray, 1836), 147.

therefore circumvents the necessity of stating whether or not he believes Hearne's account of it. But in a letter to his wife, written from Bloody Fall, he says:

> I do not think his mistake [in latitudinal measurements] willful, but the same excuse cannot be made as to his description of the Eskimaux girl clinging to his knees for his protection in his account of the bloody transaction, for the Indians assure us that he was left twenty miles or upwards in the river at a spot which they pointed out to us, and that when the war party was returning they met Hearne advancing alone having made a spear for himself by tying one leg of a pair of scissors to the end of a long pole.[6]

If Richardson's account is correct, then Hearne was not at the massacre, and the verbal picture he painted of an Inuit girl twisting her arms around his legs while begging for mercy never happened. Richardson added: "The Indian accounts of the transaction . . . agree so well with each other that I believe it."

And Richardson wasn't alone. Another member of Franklin's expedition, George Back, wrote in his field journal that "the most interesting part" of Hearne's journal "I imagine to be unfounded."

It seems, then, that Hearne embellished his narrative to suit popular tastes.

Literature scholar Robin McGrath has studied the legends of the Inuinnait, the Inuit group living nearest Bloody Fall, for any Indigenous version of the massacre story, and found none. She

---

[6] Letter, John Richardson to Mary Richardson, C.S. Houston fonds, Series VIII, University of Saskatchewan Archives, Saskatoon, transcription Box 46, file 9; quoted in Emilie Cameron, *Far Off Metal River* (Vancouver: UBC Press, 2015), 76.

found references in some narratives to events that could have been coloured by reminiscences of the events of 1771, but no native version of the story. Perhaps such a massacre was not noteworthy in those times—there were numerous warlike acts in the past perpetrated by both sides in this traditional conflict.

Throughout his narrative, Hearne does his best to portray Matonabbee in a positive light. This is a difficult task, given the man's complicity in the acts. But Hearne tries. Towards the end of his narrative, in a chapter devoted entirely to the Chipewyan middleman, he says that "when we went to war with the Esquimaux," it was "by no means his proposal; on the contrary, he was forced into it by his countrymen." But that's the problem when a writer edits his own work: he has to remember what he has said earlier. And earlier Hearne had written that the Indians "acted on this horrid occasion with the utmost unanimity of sentiment. There was not among them the least altercation or separate opinion; all were united in the general cause, and as ready to follow where Matonabbee led, as he appeared to be ready to lead." Apologists have suggested that Matonabbee was unable to control and stop the blood lust of his fellow travellers, but that is not the case. Hearne's own words— "Matonabbee led"—damn the Chipewyan leader.

Matonabbee died by suicide in the winter of 1782–83 after the destruction of Prince of Wales Fort by the French and his realization that his livelihood and high status among his people had disappeared with the fort.

Samuel Hearne was recognized by Canada as a National Historic Person in 1920.

In 1989, Canada issued a postage stamp honouring the Indigenous leader, captioned "Matonabbee Travelling North"—certainly the only Canadian stamp to honour a mass murderer.

The Return of the Dog-Children

Parry and Lyon at Iglulik

When John Ross sailed into the waters of farthest northern Greenland in 1818, he became the first Qallunaaq to meet the isolated Inughuit—the people who would become known to explorers as the "Polar Eskimos." But his visit had been foretold by a woman of the tribe some years earlier, who prophesied that "a big boat with tall poles would come into view from the ocean." When Ross's ship, the *Isabella*, hove into view, the Inuit thought it a marvel, "a whole island of wood, which moved along the sea on wings, and in its depths had many houses and rooms full of noisy people."

In Those Days

Five men first approached the ship with some trepidation. Thinking it to be a living thing, they addressed it, calling out: "Who are you? What are you? Where do you come from?" John Ross was in the enviable position of having an interpreter on board, a Kalaaleq from Disco Bay, halfway down the west coast of Greenland, who could make himself understood by the Inughuit, although their dialects were very different. The hunters asked him, "Is it from the sun or the moon?" They imagined that each of the ship's masts was a tall man who had come to destroy them. The interpreter could not convince them that the ships were not living beings—they asked whether the ship could fly as well as swim, because they had seen it flap its wings.

Four years later, two ships hove into view in an isolated part of the Canadian Arctic, near Iglulik in Foxe Basin. The commander, William Edward Parry, in charge of the *Fury*, had been second-in-command on Ross's expedition to Greenland. He had encountered Inuit on that voyage and would now meet members of a different group, speaking a different dialect. His second-in-command in 1822 was George Francis Lyon, in charge of the *Hecla*; he had joined the Royal Navy at the tender age of thirteen, and served in North Africa from 1818 until 1820. This was his first voyage to the Arctic and his first encounter with Inuit.

The two ships had spent the previous winter at an island the explorers called Winter Island, east of Repulse Bay at the mouth of an inlet that Parry named after Lyon. It was not until February 1, with the ships firmly iced in for winter, that Inuit first visited the ships.

There is unfortunately no record of what the Inuit of Iglulik made of these two ships sailing into their waters the following summer. They would surely have heard from their fellow countrymen that spring of the ships' arrival in Foxe Basin, for spring is the season when travel is easiest in the Arctic and news travels quickly, if only to break the winter monotony. They may have been as mystified as the Inughuit had been a few years earlier. Or they may have already heard of such vessels from Inuit even farther to the south who were familiar with Hudson's Bay Company vessels, which travelled to Churchill and sometimes plied the waters north from there to Marble Island to trade.

But whether or not they were familiar with ships didn't matter— once the ships had freed themselves from the clutches of the ice at Winter Island and reached Iglulik, the Inuit quickly discerned Parry's reason for having come to their shores. John Barrow, the powerful second secretary of the Admiralty, had dispatched Parry and Lyon to search for a passage west—the elusive Northwest Passage. John Ross had earlier bungled an attempt to find the passage through Lancaster Sound, earning Barrow's ire. Parry and Lyon would now search for it in the little-known waters of Foxe Basin. But the Inuit knew none of that. They had their own ideas to explain the presence of these newcomers in their waters.

The clue to their deciphering of Parry's purpose in coming to their land was their observation that he collected human skulls on the island. "We were not a little surprised to find also a number of human skulls lying about," Parry wrote, adding that he was "inclined to add some of them to our collections." The Inuit helped him in this task. They "went eagerly about to look for them, and tumbled, perhaps the craniums of some of their own relations, into our bag."

The white men, the Inuit believed, were searching for the skulls of their own ancestors.

In Those Days

In Inuit legend, Uinigumasuittuq—the one who didn't want to marry—was a young Inuit woman who refused to accede to the attentions of a succession of suitors. There are numerous versions of this tale. In one, her father, in frustration at her rejection of all potential husbands, decreed that she would therefore marry her dog. The father took her and her dog-husband to the island of Qikiqtaarjuk, where she gave birth to a litter of babies. A garrulous old woman named Orulo told the folklorist Knud Rasmussen in 1922: "She gave birth to a whole litter, some as dogs and some in right human form."

Orulo continued, "Those of her children that were born in right human form she placed on an *alaq*: a piece of sole leather that goes under the sole of the *kamik* proper, and these she sent drifting over to land. From these it is said, are descended all the Itqiliit, the Chipewyan." By extension, these were therefore the ancestors of all Indians.

Then she set her dog-children on a boot sole and, after placing three stems of grass upright on it, set them adrift, saying, "You shall be skillful in the making of weapons." The stems of grass transformed themselves into masts, and the boot sole became a sailing ship.

There are many variations to the legend. But significantly, in one of them, Uinigumasuittuq tells her departing dog-progeny, "You will come back by ship."

This legend and its variants are known throughout the eastern Inuit world. Uinigumasuittuq became the powerful woman at the bottom of the sea who controlled the hunters' access to sea mammals and could wreak havoc and hunger on Inuit unless visited and placated by shamans. In some places she was known as Sanna (a name since corrupted as Sedna), in others as Arnaaluk Takannaaluk, and in still others as Nuliajuk or Nerrivik.

Parry's skull-collecting took on particular meaning for the Iglulingmiut (the people of Iglulik). The island of Qikiqtaarjuk, where Uinigumasuittuq had given birth, was by then no longer an island, isostatic rebound having caused it to join with the main island of Iglulik. But the conclusion was inescapable—the legendary dog-children had returned. Parry was clearly searching for the skull of his mother! In fact, according to what respected elder Rosie Iqallijuq told writer Dorothy Eber in 1998, he found what he was looking for. "Paarii and his people came around here for the skull of their mother," said Rosie, "and took it from Qikiqtaarjuk—but we didn't see that!"

Parry may never have known of the Inuit interpretation of his arrival and his activities. But it was clear to the Inuit. He was the realization of Uinigumasuittuq's prophesy that her dog-children would return by ship. Despite the language barrier that separated the two races, the Inuit viewed Parry as their kin. This may explain why relations between the Inuit and their Qallunaat visitors remained friendly for most of that winter.

* * *

Parry and Lyon didn't discover the Northwest Passage, only a narrow and impractical ice-choked strait leading west, which Parry named Fury and Hecla Strait after the expedition's two ships. Parry himself described his venture as "unsuccessful, but, I trust & believe, not discreditable."

That assessment depends entirely on whether one listens to Inuit or Qallunaat accounts. Both explorers went to great lengths to establish friendly relations with the local Inuit. Indeed, their instructions from the Admiralty were, should they meet any "Esquimaux," to endeavor "to cultivate a friendship with them, by making them presents of such articles as you may be supplied with, and which may be useful or agreeable to them." Parry and Lyon were well-stocked with trade goods—tobacco, food, beads, cloth—and were generous with the Inuit; the Inuit in turn were helpful to the expedition, drawing maps, providing and repairing clothing, and welcoming the Qallunaat into their homes. Presciently, the explorers provided only one man with a gun and enough ammunition for only one season; they did not want to present more lest the Inuit become dependent on rifles but then have no source of more ammunition. Both men established a rapport with the Inuit and were apparently genuinely interested in them, their customs, and their language. Both produced books that were remarkable for their level of ethnographic detail. Lyon in particular was a talented illustrator—his drawings formed the basis for the illustrations in both men's volumes—and apparently immersed himself in Inuit life, going so far as to have a woman make a two-inch tattoo on his skin.

Sadly, after an uneventful winter, the expedition ended on a sour note. An Inuit man named Oo-oo-took was accused of stealing a shovel from Parry's ship. Parry retaliated by banishing Inuit from visiting the *Fury*. Some time later Oo-oo-took, who had been an infrequent visitor in the past, managed to be onboard visiting the assistant surgeon, Mr. Skeoch, in his cabin. Learning from Skeoch that the theft of the shovel had been discovered, he feared that the man had "dived into his thoughts." Oo-oo-took went ashore and returned shortly with the shovel. Despite the return of the pilfered item, Parry decided to administer naval discipline and make an example of the man. He conducted what was in effect a "show trial" and had the unfortunate man flogged.

Parry brought several Inuit on board as witnesses, then

> I ordered him to be stripped and seized up in their presence, and to receive a dozen lashes on the back with a cat-o'-nine tails. The instant this was over, his countrymen called out very earnestly, "Timun, timunna," (That's right, that's right,) and seemed much relieved from the fright they had before been in while the fate of the thief seemed doubtful; but in three minutes after not one of them was to be found near the ships. . . . This example proved just what we desired; in less than eight-and-forty hours, men, women, and children came to the ships with the same confidence as before, always [verbally] abusing Oo-oo-took, pronouncing themselves and us uncommonly good people, but evidently more cautious than before of really incurring our displeasure.[7]

But Parry likely misunderstood the reaction of the Inuit onlookers. The utterance he quotes was probably really *"Taima, taima,"* which, in the context, likely meant "Enough, enough." Their pleasantness when they returned forty-eight hours later was a form of caution in the presence of a "friend" who had begun to act irrationally.

The experience of the flogging, passed down through oral history to succeeding generations of Iglulingmiut, blighted Inuit memory of the expedition. Inuit told Charles Francis Hall in 1864 that Oo-oo-took, in fact, had been a "superior" *angakkuq*

---

[7] William Edward Parry, *Journal of a Second Voyage for the Discovery of a North-West Passage from the Atlantic to the Pacific* (London: John Murray, 1824), 412.

In Those Days

(shaman). In the account the Inuit preserved, Parry had Oo-oo-took taken to a place between decks where his hands were firmly tied to the mast. "Then two guns were loaded and fired at him. The balls did not hit him, but one passed close to his head and lodged in the mast. The other ball went close to his loins, but did not injure him. The guns were so near his body that the powder felt hot. . . . Then Parry caused him to be whipped with something that was made of ropes with knots in them." This is a perfect description of a cat-o'-nine-tails. The Inuit witnesses wanted to help Oo-oo-took, but he said, "Let the Kob-lu-nas [Qallunaat] try to kill me; they cannot, for I am an an-nat-ko [angakkuq]." His hands were untied and the Qallunaat tried to cut his head and hands off with swords, but they were unsuccessful: "Every time a blow was struck, the extreme end of the knife came close to Oo-oo-took's throat; occasionally the blade came just above the crown of his head, and when the attempt was made to cut off his hands the long knife came down very near his wrists; but after all, he was uninjured because he was a very god an-nat-ko." Some of the blows hit him, making deep gashes in his throat, head, and wrists, but each time the knife was removed the wounds mirac-ulously healed. After that, he was thrown into the hold for two days and two nights. When he called upon his spirits to split the ship in two, great cracking noises were heard; Inuit believe that is why he was finally released.

But Oo-oo-took was not yet finished with Parry. He had a revenge to exact on him and all his fellow dog-children. He was, after all, a powerful shaman. Elder Herve Paniaq recorded his knowledge of the events of so long ago, the story of the shaman's curse, for the Igloolik Oral History Project, and said, "When they were done with him, he blew them away and told them never to return again." Another Iglulingmiutaq, Pauli Kunnuk, noted that "the Inuk made it not possible for ships ever to return on account of the ice. . . . It is said that through shamanism it was no longer possible for ships to make it here."

It is perhaps significant that, after the pronouncement of this curse and the banishment from the island of the dog-children, dogs were named after Parry and Lyon, and later after Hall.

There are other versions of the story that don't mention the theft of a shovel. In a version recorded in 1991, Rosie Iqallijuq said, "I heard at the time when Paarii wintered, there was a shaman who was jealous over his wife when she started to go around with some white people. When the ships departed it is said that with the help of his helping spirit he blew the ship away so that no other ship can ever make it back to Iglulik."

Indeed, there may have been some truth to this version. In December of 1864, through his interpreter Tookoolito, Charles Francis Hall was interviewing an elderly Inuit woman, Erktua, about Parry's experiences. In his journal he recorded that Erktua had been the lover of Parry and then Lyon, noting "Especially Private!" in the margin: "Erktua furthermore says that when Parry found out she had slept with Lyon, and Lyon learned that she had done the same with Parry, they became jealous; and for this Erktua ever after refused to sleep with either again." But this did not slow down the red-blooded Lyon. Erktua claimed that when the expedition departed, two Inuit sisters were pregnant with his children.

Indeed, it is possible that the shovel had not been stolen but had been given to someone as a gift, perhaps in return for sexual favours. Royal Navy ships were rife with such gift-giving wherever in the world sailors went ashore.

In Those Days

For some, the shaman's curse was not just to prevent ships from arriving at Iglulik, but to prevent any white men from arriving there by any means. When Alfred Tremblay reached the island overland from Pond Inlet by dog sled in 1913, the Inuit viewed the curse as having been lifted. The visit of Hall to the island in May of 1868 doesn't seem to have counted, perhaps because he was there so briefly, whereas Tremblay remained for a number of days, enough apparently to break the long-standing spell. While there he exhibited his own bizarre behaviour; Rosie Iqallijuq recalled that "he had a pistol so with it he shot the island of Iglulik as he walked around the shoreline. After he had shot the island he said that Iglulik was dead and that a ship will now be able to get to the island." Nonetheless, it would still be a number of years before any ship reached Iglulik.

It's sometimes been written that the shaman cursed the island of Iglulik. But that's not the case. The curse was on the white men—the dog-children—to prevent them from reaching the island again, because of their irrational behaviour and their humiliation of a powerful shaman. Those vindictive actions, apparently over the matter of a shovel that may have been stolen and then returned, were unnecessary and destroyed the rapport that had built between the people of two quite different backgrounds, who nonetheless had considered themselves kin.

Parry's
Medallions

It is well known that the federal government initiated a system of disks with identifying numbers for Inuit in 1941. Each disk was stamped with a unique number. This system remained in place until 1972 in the Northwest Territories, longer in Nunavik.

What is little known is the fact that a different type of disk, or medallion, was issued in the eastern Canadian Arctic over a century earlier. They were issued to Inuit, but they were not used for identification purposes.

In 1822 William Edward Parry's two expedition ships, the *Fury* and *Hecla*, were anchored off Winter Island in Foxe Basin. Inuit visited the ships for the first time on February 1. On the fifteenth of that month, Parry had intended to go hunting with an Inuk named Okotook, but strong winds kept them stormbound aboard ship. Instead Parry decided that this would be a good day to put in place his plan to have the Inuit help in letting other non-Inuit travellers—if there were any—know of the British expedition's general location in the Arctic.

In fact, another expedition under the British Admiralty was in northern North America at the same time. This was John Franklin's expedition, which had left England in 1819. Its purpose was to travel overland to the mouth of the Coppermine River and from there travel eastward along the Arctic coast. That expedition was still in the field when Parry's was dispatched, and the Admiralty held some hope that the two expeditions might meet in the Arctic.

Parry recognized that the Inuit travelled by land and sea more extensively than he would be able to do from his iced-in position in Foxe Basin. Thus his plan. He gave the Inuit men "large round medallions of sheet copper" on each of which was punched the message, "H. B. M. S. Fury and Hecla, All well, A.D. 1822." These were manufactured onboard from sheet copper that he carried. They were suspended by a piece of "white line"—a string— around the men's necks. The Inuit were told to show them to any "Kabloona people," or Qallunaat, they might meet in the future. By questioning the Inuit, the "Kabloona people" would know where Parry's expedition had been located.

But there was another purpose in giving out these markers, which William Hooper, purser aboard the *Fury*, made clear in his journal: "Should they go Southward and see other Europeans; they were told that in the event of them doing so, and showing the medals, they would be certain of being kindly received." The implication is that, should these Inuit travel or trade as far south as the Hudson's Bay Company post at Churchill, or meet traders from Churchill north of that post in summer, and show the medallions, the traders would convey that information to England with the next post, thereby letting the Admiralty know that the expedition had been safe in 1822, if it had not returned in the interim.

Parry also gave similar medallions, of a smaller size and bearing only the words "Fury and Hecla, 1822," to the women. The fact that he refers to these as "ornaments" indicates that the women probably requested them as decorations. One of these even turns up in a short story, "The Traveller," in Mary Martha Sherwood's 1842 book *The Holiday Keepsake*, in which the narrator tells that "amongst the Esquimaux women who came to our ship, was one who had a medallion of sheet copper fastened by a piece of white line round her neck."

George Lyon, in command of the *Hecla*, records that, when Okotook and his wife Iligliak visited him, the man was wearing his copper medal. Lyon confirmed that the hope was that "owing to the wandering life of the Eskimaux, some one of these ornaments might, through our factories, reach England before our return."

No example of these unique disks or medallions is known to exist today, neither in an archive nor a private collection. One wonders though. Each one had a hole in the middle so that it could be easily worn as a necklace. At some point in the 1800s, Inuit women became enamoured of fastening decorative objects to their clothing, especially to parkas or *amautiit*. These objects included coins and even spoon bowls, which were perforated for this specific use. The Parry medallions would have made ideal adornments for clothing articles. Were they used as such? One wonders if an example of Parry's medallions may yet turn up in an archaeological site or ancient grave.

"A Greater Instance of Courage has not been Recorded"

Tatannuaq, the Peacemaker

Sir John Franklin was as inept an explorer as the Arctic has ever seen. The commander of an expedition of two ships that left England in 1847 to search for the fabled Northwest Passage, he gives a whole new meaning to the word "lost." For Franklin became lost not just in the sense that he didn't know where he was—in fact he may very well have known exactly where he was—no, Franklin become irrevocably and irretrievably lost, so that no one else knew where he was and no one could succeed in rescuing him.

John Franklin, born in England, joined the Royal Navy at the age of fourteen. But in May of 1815, with the Napoleonic Wars drawing to an end, he found himself discharged. Three years later, the Admiralty, under the determined leadership of its second secretary, John Barrow, became interested in exploring the Arctic and finding a passage to the Pacific, either through what we now know as the Northwest Passage or over the North Pole. Franklin was given command of a ship, the *Trent*, as part of a two-ship expedition under the command of David Buchan. They attempted, unsuccessfully, to cross the Arctic Ocean but were stopped, prophetically, by impenetrable ice north of Spitsbergen. Franklin and impassable ice—it was a theme that would recur.

In 1819 he left for the Arctic again, this time in charge of a land expedition sent by the Admiralty to explore the north coast of America eastward from the mouth of the Coppermine River to Hudson Bay. Franklin and his party sailed to York Factory on Hudson Bay, then continued on to Cumberland House, a Hudson's Bay Company post in what is now Saskatchewan, where they spent part of the winter. Franklin and George Back left on snowshoes in January for Fort Chipewyan. Another party followed later in the spring with supplies. In July, once the parties were reunited, they proceeded down the Slave River and across Great Slave Lake to Fort Providence, a North West Company post. The manager there recruited Indians to guide Franklin and his party to the Coppermine River as well as to hunt for them.

The Indians in question were the Yellowknives, a northwestern band of Chipewyan. Franklin called them the "Copper Indians." They ranged from the east arm of Great Slave Lake to

In Those Days

the Coppermine River, along the shores of which copper was said to exist. Both names by which the tribe was known derived from the alleged presence of this metal.

On July 30, 1820, the leader of the largest band of Yellowknives arrived at Fort Providence to meet Franklin, whom he had agreed to assist. This was Akaitcho—the name means "Big Foot" in the local Athabascan language—and he led a group comprising about forty men and boys. (Curiously, the number of females is not mentioned.)

His arrival was designed to impress. Franklin recorded it this way:

> On landing at the fort, the chief assumed a very grave aspect, and walked . . . with a measured and dignified step, looking neither to the right nor to the left . . . but preserved the same immoveability of countenance until he reached the hall, and was introduced to the officers. When he had smoked his pipe, drank a small portion of spirits and water himself, and issued a glass to each of his companions, who had seated themselves on the floor, he commenced his harangue, by mentioning the circumstances that led to his agreeing to accompany the Expedition. . . . He was rejoiced . . . to see such great chiefs on his lands, his tribe were poor, but they loved the white men who had been their benefactors; and he hoped that our visit would be productive of much good to them.[8]

The neighbouring Dogrib and Hare Indians feared Akaitcho. He was a "fierce and aggressive leader" who had driven them from

---

[8] John Franklin, *Narrative of a Journey to the Shores of the Polar Sea in the Years 1819, 20, 21, and 22* (London: John Murray, 1823), 202.

parts of their traditional hunting range, stolen furs and women, and on occasion murdered them.

Franklin was to learn that Akaitcho was stubborn and unyielding where the interests of his tribe were concerned. Once the journey was underway, the man resisted suggestions that they should reach the Arctic coast that season, and as a result Franklin and his party passed the winter of 1820–21 at Fort Enterprise. He had arranged that two Inuit interpreters from Hudson Bay join his party there and accompany him to the Coppermine. Therefore two Inuit, Tatannuaq and Hiutiruq, travelled overland from Hudson Bay through Great Slave Lake and joined Franklin in January of 1821.

Tatannuaq had been born and raised about two hundred miles north of Churchill. From 1812 to 1814 and again the following winter, he worked for the Hudson's Bay Company at its Churchill post, where he learned English and the skills of an interpreter. He returned to his Inuit community in 1816, took a wife two years later, and fathered three sons.

Franklin always referred to Tatannuaq as Augustus and Hiutiruq as Junius. Of Tatannuaq, he wrote that he "speaks English sufficiently to make himself understood on common subjects." Later he elaborated, with an opinion of both men: "The Esquimaux interpreter [Tatannuaq] and his companion are very good tempered men and appear to be quite happy both in their present situation and at the prospect of the proposed journey. We find they understand many of the words which have been read to them from the Labrador Moravian Testament and are therefore induced to suppose there may be such a general similarity of dialect among the different tribes of Esquimaux, that they will experience little difficulty in comprehending the people we may meet on the coast."

In Those Days

Tatannuaq had one other remarkable ability. He had learned to speak Cree at Churchill. The Chipewyan chief, Akaitcho, and many of his colleagues who were at Fort Enterprise also spoke some Cree, a language they used in their interactions with Cree middlemen in the fur trade.

The two Inuit accompanied Franklin's party to the Arctic coast and were invaluable in his exploration of the coast to the east. But on the return journey to Fort Enterprise, many of the party died of starvation; Hiutiruq disappeared while hunting and was never found. Junius Lake in the Northwest Territories, between Great Bear Lake and the Coppermine River, was named in his honour. Tatannuaq also became separated from the rest of the party, but eventually returned safely to the fort.

With the end of Franklin's first overland expedition, Tatannuaq returned to Churchill in 1822, where he was again employed by the Hudson's Bay Company. That summer at York Factory and again the following year at Churchill, he acted as interpreter for the missionary John West, but there is no indication that he converted to Christianity.

* * *

George Simpson, the outspoken governor of the Hudson's Bay Company, had little regard for Franklin, his failure to adapt to Arctic conditions, and his inflexible approach. He wrote that Franklin "has not the physical powers required for the labour of moderate voyaging in this country; he must have three meals per diem, tea is indispensable, and with the utmost exertion he cannot walk above eight miles in one day, so that it does not follow [that] if those gentlemen are unsuccessful that the difficulties are insurmountable."

But Franklin had shown one quality that impressed the Admiralty: courage. Perhaps they didn't recognize the fine line between that sterling quality and its tragic counterpart— foolhardiness.

And so in 1825 John Franklin returned to the Arctic on another overland expedition. In the spring of that year he hired Tatannuaq again as interpreter, along with another Inuk, Ouligbuck. They joined Franklin at Methy (now Methye) Portage in what is now Saskatchewan. The party travelled via the river system to the Mackenzie and on to the shores of Great Bear Lake, where they wintered at Fort Franklin, named for himself.

On June 26, 1826, they set out down the Great Bear and Mackenzie rivers for the coast in four eight-metre boats. The parties divided at the head of the Mackenzie Delta, and Tatannuaq accompanied Franklin's and George Back's party to the west. On July 7, they unexpectedly encountered several hundred Inuit. At one point, Franklin and Back counted seventy-three kayaks and five umiaqs, with more still arriving. Franklin prepared gifts for the Inuit, but unfortunately they had not approached with friendly intent. They pillaged both boats and hauled Franklin's boat ashore in the shallow water. Franklin's sixteen men were seriously outnumbered. Tatannuaq was active in attempting to halt the plunder, and "endeavoured to stop their proceedings until he was quite hoarse with speaking." Finally Back got his boat afloat again and his crew levelled their guns at the Inuit, who immediately retreated. These events did not augur well for the success of the rest of Franklin's mission.

The boats had barely cleared the mouth of the river when they ran aground again in shallow water, about 150 yards offshore. A party of eight Inuit appeared and requested that Tatannuaq come ashore. Franklin at first refused to allow it, but Tatannuaq insisted on going ashore unarmed, "as he was also desirous of reproving them for their Conduct."

Franklin's own words tell best about that meeting:

> He intrepidly went and a complete explanation took place. He pointed out that it was entirely forbearance on our part that many of them had not been certainly killed, as we were provided with the means of firing at a long distance. He told them that we were come here entirely for their benefit. In his own country he told them they were formerly in the same state of want as themselves, but that since the white people had come among them, they were supplied with every useful article. . . . He was well clothed, got what he required and was most comfortable. . . . The English love the Esquimaux and all Indians, and are kind to them and so they will be to you if you receive them as you ought. I repeat they are not afraid of you and can kill you a long way off if they choose. . . . If you had killed any of the white men I would have shot you. This speech was addressed to upwards of forty persons who had now assembled round him and all of them with knives, and he quite unarmed. A greater instance of courage has not been I think recorded.[9]

Tatannuaq's bravery mollified the Inuit, who, he reported, expressed their sorrow and regret. They claimed that they had never seen white men before and that the material goods they saw

---

[9] John Franklin, "Captain Franklin's Journal to October 1825," in Richard Davis (ed.), *Sir John Franklin's Journals and Correspondence: The Second Arctic Land Expedition 1825–1827* (Toronto: The Champlain Society, 1998), 205.

were so "new and desirable to them" that they could not resist the temptation to steal them. There is little doubt that Tatannuaq's skill prevented loss of life on both sides.

After a survey of a portion of the coast, Franklin's party began its return to Fort Franklin. This time the Inuit they encountered were friendly, some even warning Tatannuaq of the harmful intentions of others. When the reportedly treacherous Inuit approached, ostensibly to return pilfered items, Franklin refused to allow them to get close, and fired a shot in front of their bows.

When the expedition reached Norway House in June of 1827, Tatannuaq's employment was at an end, and he wept at the separation.

Tatannuaq had a good reputation with the Hudson's Bay Company, so much so that in 1829 he was called upon to travel to Ungava Bay in what is now Nunavik to assist in the establishment of a new trading post, Fort Chimo, at the site of present-day Kuujjuaq. He remained there for four years but in 1833 was summoned to join an expedition led by his old friend, George Back, in search of the missing expedition of John Ross. After reaching York Factory, Tatannuaq set out to walk with two other men from Hudson Bay to Fort Reliance at the eastern end of Great Slave Lake to join the explorer. They lost their way, and the other men, a French-Canadian and an Iroquois, turned back, but Tatannuaq insisted on continuing. He forged ahead with only ten pounds of pemmican, no gun, and no bow and arrow. A party of Indians was sent out from Fort Resolution to search for him, and on June 3 his body was discovered only about ten miles from that fort. He had frozen to death in a snowstorm.

George Back, who, along with Dr. John Richardson, had participated in both of Franklin's overland expeditions, was distraught at the news. "Such was the miserable end of poor Augustus!" he wrote, "a faithful, disinterested, kind-hearted creature, who had won the regard not of myself only, but I may add of Sir John Franklin and Dr. Richardson also." Augustus Lake in the Northwest Territories, just south of Junius Lake, is named after him.

First Encounter

The Nattilingmiut Meet John Ross

I n 1923 the Danish-Greenlandic explorer and ethnographer Knud Rasmussen spent the better part of the year among the Nattilingmiut as part of his major ethnographic expedition, the Fifth Thule Expedition across Arctic North America. One group of the Nattilingmiut was the Arviligjuarmiut, the people of Pelly Bay. From them, he heard a story of their first encounter with Qallunaat, a meeting that had taken place almost a century earlier. Rasmussen wrote:

> The Arviligjuarmiut still had many recollections of their first meeting with white men, and the sober manner in which they told of these experiences, now almost a hundred years old, is good evidence of how reliable the Eskimos can be as narrators. . . .

In Those Days

They tell that [a] ship was first seen early in the winter by a man named Aviluktoq, who was out sealing. When he caught sight of the great ship lying like a rock out in the middle of a small bay, his curiosity at first made him approach to see what it could be, for he had never noticed it before. But when he saw the ship's high masts he thought it was a great spirit and fled. All that evening and night the men considered what they should do, but as they were afraid that the big spirit might destroy them if they did not forestall it, they set out next day to attack it, armed with harpoons and bows.

Then they discovered that human figures were walking about it, and they hid behind a block of ice to see what sort of people these could be. They had heard of kinsmen who in far distant lands had met white men, but they themselves had never done so. However, the figures round the ship had also seen them and made their way over the ice towards the ice blocks behind which they were hiding. They saw at once that the strangers must be the famous white men of whom they had heard so much talk and who were said to have come from the offspring of a girl in their own country and a dog.

All the Arviligjuarmiut now wished to show that they were not afraid, and came out from their place of concealment. The white men at once laid their weapons on the ice, and the Eskimos followed suit. The meeting was a cordial one, with both embraces and what each party took to be assurances of friendship, for of course they could not understand a word of each other's tongue. The Eskimos went along to this great, wonderful ship and received precious gifts such as nails, sewing needles and knives, in fact everything that they could not get in the country itself. And the white men seemed to have such an abundance of wood that they could even live in it—indeed, however incredible it may sound, they lived in a hollowed-out floating island of wood that was full of iron and everything else that was precious in their own country.

This was the first meeting. Later on they often came together and the Eskimos vied with each other in accompanying them on journeys and assisting them in a region that they knew inside out. They were very fond of going on journeys with them. One of the big chiefs on the ship they called Agluukkaq (he who takes the long strides), for he always seemed to be in a hurry and was impatient to advance quickly on all his travels. . . .

When the strangers went away they left large quantities of wood, iron, nails, anchor chains, iron hoops and other valuables which to this day are used for knives, arrow heads, harpoon heads, salmon leisters, caribou lances, and hooks. Once a mast drifted ashore, and of it they made sledges, kayaks and harpoons. The mast was split up by first making saws of barrel hoops; this took the whole of the summer and autumn, but time was not of much consequence if only they were able to utilize the valuable wood.[10]

Rasmussen commented that "so many years afterwards they preserve the traditions of their experiences with unembellished and sober reliability." Rasmussen was well-read in Arctic history. He

---

[10] Knud Rasmussen, *The Netsilik Eskimos: Social Life and Spiritual Culture. Report of the Fifth Thule Expedition 1921–24*, Vol. VIII, No. 1 (Copenhagen: Gyldendalske Boghandel, 1931), 28.

In Those Days

immediately knew who the white men of the long-ago expedition were. He added that, if the reports of that expedition were studied, "the ancient verbal traditions will be found to be in the best agreement with the books."

* * *

In 1818, after John Ross returned from his voyage to Baffin Bay, in which he entered Lancaster Sound—the entrance to the Northwest Passage—then turned back, believing it blocked by mountains, he was roundly criticized in Britain for his mistake, for those in the accompanying ship and many on his own claimed not to have seen the looming mountain range at all. In particular, the all-powerful John Barrow, second secretary of the Admiralty, took a dislike to Ross, effectively blackballing him. His career went into a hiatus until 1929, when he secured the backing of a wealthy gin merchant, Sir Felix Booth.

John Ross and his nephew, James Clark Ross, left London in May of that year in the *Victory*, with the intention of finally finding the elusive Northwest Passage. Their initial difficulties were with the vessel's steam engine rather than with ice. After passing through Lancaster Sound with no difficulty and steaming south through Prince Regent Inlet, they passed the strait later known as Bellot Strait without seeing it and continued along the coast of what Ross would name Boothia Peninsula, after his benefactor. Late in the season, with ice forming, they found a wintering place, naming it also after their patron, Felix Harbour.

Ross was unimpressed by his surroundings. Indeed, he wrote one of the dreariest descriptions of an Arctic landscape on record: "The voyager may be a painter, or he may be a poet; but his talents at description will here be of no value to him; unless he has the hardihood to invent what there is not to see." Nature here, he said, was "void of every thing to which the face of a country owes its charms." One wonders what he would have written had he known at that time that his imprisonment in the ice of the Arctic would last for three more winters.

On January 9, 1830, Ross's crew had visitors. Four Inuit were seen about a mile distant. Ross and his men, carrying guns, approached them. They saw that each of the Inuit carried a knife and a spear. Ross shouted to them, "Tima, tima," which, he claimed, was "the word of salutation between meeting tribes." The Inuit shouted back in return. The white men threw down their guns. Immediately the Inuit threw down their weapons.

James Clark Ross, the man whom the Inuit would name Agluukkaq (the long strider), claimed some familiarity with the Inuit language, having spent two winters near Iglulik with William Edward Parry's expedition almost a decade earlier. Through him, the British were able to learn something of this group, which numbered thirty-six. They quickly found out that, in addition to their native knives, these Inuit also possessed knives tipped with iron. Indeed, the cautious natives, although they had made a great show of throwing down their weapons, each had an iron-tipped knife concealed within his clothing; one was even made of an English clasp knife, which still bore the maker's marks. Ross quickly concluded that "this was a proof of communication with the tribes that trade with Europeans."

Ross invited the men aboard his ship and gave them a tour. They wanted to know the name of each thing they saw and its usage. They sampled the preserved meats that Ross offered them from his stores, but didn't fancy them. On deck, a fiddler produced a violin, and the Inuit joined the crew in dancing and, Ross thought, showed a great aptitude for music.

Ross observed that all the natives were well dressed, mostly in caribou skins. His published account describes their clothing in detail, and concludes that "with this immense superstructure of clothes, they seemed a much larger people than they really were."

This first encounter between the Rosses and the Nattilingmiut augured well for the future. John Ross and some of his men accompanied the Inuit for about two miles when they left. When they parted, Ross marked a spot on the ice and indicated that they should meet again there the following day. He would have many encounters with Inuit during the next three winters, most of them pleasant, but a few of them marked by discord.

He wrote of this first meeting:

This was a most satisfactory day; for we had given up all expectations of meeting inhabitants in this place; while we knew that it was to the natives that we must look for such geographical information as would assist us. . . . It was for philosophers to interest themselves in speculating on a horde so small, and so secluded, occupying so apparently hopeless a country, so barren, so wild, and so repulsive; and yet enjoying the most perfect vigour, the most well-fed health, and all else that here constitutes, not merely wealth, but the opulence of luxury; since they were so amply furnished with provisions, as with every other thing that could be necessary to their wants.[11]

---

[11] Sir John Ross, *Narrative of a Second Voyage in Search of a North-West Passage* (London: A. W. Webster, 1835), 248.

Collected Writings on Arctic History

* * *

Recollections documented by Knud Rasmussen in 1923 corroborated and enhanced much of what John Ross wrote about his meeting with the Nattilingmiut nine decades earlier—the same story in its broad outline, but told from two different cultural perspectives.

Twenty-four years after Rasmussen passed through the area, another version of the story was told to Lorenz Learmonth, a fur trader with the Hudson's Bay Company, who had a passionate interest in local history. Learmonth spoke Inuktitut well, as many traders did in those days when posts were isolated and visitors few. He spent much of his time excavating archaeological sites and recording Inuit lore.

In 1947 he recorded a story told to him some years earlier by Ohokto, a Nattilingmiutaq, whose ancestors had passed the story down from generation to generation. In many ways the account verifies the version collected by Rasmussen. There are differences, however. It is a much richer and more detailed account—Learmonth had the advantage of having lived and worked with the Inuit in the central Canadian Arctic for many years, whereas Rasmussen passed through the area comparatively quickly. Rasmussen recorded the main character's name as Aviluktoq, Learmonth as Ableelooktook. (I will use Rasmussen's spelling throughout; his background in Greenlandic allowed him to record names more accurately than most traders.) Learmonth told Ohokto's story this way:

One day in the middle of winter many years ago, off the north shore of Lord Mayor Bay . . . a number of natives

73

were out aglu hunting [breathing-hole sealing] . . . when one, Aviluktoq, wandered far to the south of where his companions were hunting, led by his hunting dog straining eagerly at its leash. Aviluktoq believed the animal had scented a bear. But suddenly he pulled up short because what was that he saw ahead?—strange sight indeed—what appeared to be a house, but not such as he was familiar with, with smoke pouring from its roof and many human beings moving around in its vicinity.

Not knowing what this strange sight could mean, Aviluktoq was greatly frightened, and without delay took to his heels and made back to the snow village, situated well back in the bay. There he arrived as darkness set in, and just as his companions also returned from their hunting.

Soon he had told of his discovery, upon which the whole population of the village quickly gathered together in the large village dance house to discuss the matter. Here the principal angakkuq . . . donned his main belt of charms and his cape, made of pieces of white deer belly hide, and without delay got to work. He first took a large deerskin and pegged it to the west wall inside the dance house so as to leave the lower side resting partly on the floor. He then obtained a pair of deerskin pants from one of the men and carefully laid them out on the floor behind the deerskin curtain with legs pointing towards the back wall, then crawled in behind the curtain, ordered all qulliq [stone lamp] lights to be extinguished, and the séance was on.

As the crowd of scared men, women and children huddled together and anxiously waited in the darkened dance house, the angakkuq got in touch with his familiar spirits and through them with all the other spirits that mattered. . . .

When all the spirits had gathered together under the curtain, they informed the angakkuq that the strangers seen by Aviluktoq were white men and that they would welcome a visit by the Eskimos. Then the spirits of the white men themselves arrived behind the curtain and invited all the Eskimos to visit their camp . . . the following day.

Thus it was the entire population of the village turned out by daybreak the following morning and proceeded to Felix Harbour. When they came in sight of the house [the *Victory* under canvas covers and dismantled] they halted and sent forward Nalungituk to await the arrival of some of the white men who could be seen approaching without knives or spears or anything in their hands. Soon they were all on friendly terms with each other and moved over close to the house, where the boss of the white men came forward and greeted them.[12]

Ohokto's story also presented a side of John Ross—his temper—that Ross sanitized out of his own published version and that did not make it into Rasmussen's published version. Learmonth recorded:

After the second round of greeting was over, the boss [John Ross, presumably] enquired for the man who had been seen near the camp on the previous day as he wished to make him a present. Whereupon Aviluktoq stepped forward and

---

[12] L. A. Learmonth, "Ross Meets the Netchiliks," *The Beaver* (September 1948): 10–11.

went with him into the house. Once inside the boss handed him an ulu, a woman's knife, which offended Aviluktoq, because he was a man and a great hunter. What did he want with a woman's knife? So he pointed to a hand saw which was hanging on a nail and indicated that he would prefer that to the ulu. This in turn made the boss angry, and he thereupon took the ulu back from Aviluktoq, refused him the saw and chased him out of the house.[13]

---

[13] Ibid., 11.

A Wooden Leg
for Tulluahiu

One of the men John Ross met on his first encounter with the Nattilingmiut on the ice off Boothia Peninsula was a man, Tulluahiu, being pulled on a sled by his relatives. He had lost a leg in a hunting accident. A polar bear had ripped his leg from his body just below the knee, and he had very nearly lost his life. But this didn't prevent him from playing a part in the first encounter. By the time Ross's party had reached the group of Inuit on the ice, Tulluahiu was standing, supported by two other men, a long knife concealed behind his back. He held it there until it was apparent that these white men were no threat. (I am using Ross's spelling of Inuit names throughout.)

Two days later, Tulluahiu visited Ross's ship again, drawn on a sled by his friend Tiagashu. The temperature was minus 35 degrees Fahrenheit.

In Those Days

Ross took some interest in the unfortunate amputee, and his name appears many times in the explorer's narrative of his expedition. Indeed, Ross referred to the man and his family as "the most remarkable family we met with." Tulluahiu was about forty years old, and about five feet eight inches in height. He was a little fatter than others of his countrymen, probably because of his immobility.

Ross felt compassion for the man and asked the ship's doctor to examine the stump that remained of his severed leg. The doctor found the wound to be well healed and the stump to be sound because the injury was an old one. The knee, he thought, was in good shape. Ross then sent for the carpenter, Chimham Thomas, who measured the man up for a wooden leg.

The construction of an artificial leg would take a few days. Tulluahiu remained on the ship for the rest of that day, and he and Tiagashu drew some maps of the surrounding area for Ross.

Three days later Tulluahiu came again, as one might do today for the preliminary fitting of a prosthetic device. The carpenter—for this had now become solely a job for a craftsman rather than a surgeon—had to determine whether the length was correct, and then put the finishing touches on his workmanship. The next day, when Tulluahiu returned, the leg was complete and the carpenter fastened it to the man, who strutted about the deck of the ship, elated at his newfound freedom. John Ross was proud of his carpenter's efforts. He wrote that he doubted "if any effort of surgery ever gave more satisfaction than was thus conferred, in reproducing a man fully serviceable once more to himself and his community." The carpenter had proudly inscribed the word *Victory*, the name of Ross's ship, on the leg.

It would take some time for Tulluahiu to become totally at ease with his new appendage. The camp where he was staying was two miles away, so when it was time to leave the ship, he removed the leg and packed it on the sled. Some time later, Ross learned, Tulluahiu was able to accompany other hunters on a seal hunt. But the carpenter, Thomas, wasn't yet satisfied with his results. He manufactured a better foot for the leg, more suitable for walking on snow, and fitted his patient with it on his next visit. On January 24, Tulluahiu proudly walked the whole distance from his camp to the ship, being by now the "master of his implement."

Some time later, Tulluahiu paid Ross another visit. He had damaged the trunk part of his wooden leg, but it was easily repaired with bands of copper. The carpenter died of scurvy before the expedition left the Arctic in 1833, but before his death he made several spare legs, which were presented to the ever-grateful Tulluahiu for future use.

There is a bizarre postscript to this act of charity. Over a hundred years later, in March of 1950, a permit was issued to Lorenz Learmonth under the Ordinance Respecting the Protection and Care of Archaeological Sites. Learmonth, a long-time employee of the Hudson's Bay Company, was an amateur archaeologist who liked to dig in the summers. Local Inuit helped him in his collecting.

That summer Learmonth's Inuit assistants excavated the grave of Tulluahiu a little west of Thom Bay. Fifty-six items were removed from the grave, "alongside of which lay the wooden leg made by John Ross's ship's carpenter." Learmonth sent all the grave goods to the Royal Ontario Museum in Toronto. There is no record of what became of the wooden leg.

"The Deep Footprints of Tired Men"

John Franklin's Lost Expedition

In the early 1800s John Franklin led two overland expeditions to explore the north coast of North America. But by the fall of 1827 he had returned to England to await the pleasure of the government in determining his next duty.

Franklin's next major posting was as lieutenant governor of Tasmania, then known as Van Diemen's Land, a penal colony south of Australia. When he returned home in 1844, he was given the command of the *Erebus* and *Terror*, to leave the following year for the Northwest Passage. At fifty-eight, he was too old for the task, and even more out of shape than when he had met George Simpson almost thirty years earlier.

Franklin's was the best-provisioned Arctic expedition to that time. His two ships carried 134 men and supplies for three years. They left England amid much fanfare and great expectations in May of 1845 and were last seen by whalers in northern Baffin Bay on July 26. And then, silence. John Franklin was never heard from again, and no trace found of his lost expedition for five years.

A huge search effort resulted—thirty expeditions during the twelve years from 1847 to 1859. In that year, on King William Island, William Hobson, a member of Francis Leopold McClintock's expedition, found a message in a cylinder at the base of a cairn. The paper had been signed by James Fitzjames, captain of the *Erebus*, and by Francis Crozier, who had been captain of the *Terror*. It presented the facts starkly: that both ships had been deserted on April 22, 1848, having been beset in the ice for over a year. It went on to say that "Sir John Franklin died on 11th June 1847; and the total loss by deaths in the Expedition has been to this date 9 officers & 15 men."

Ice had once again proven to be John Franklin's nemesis. The rest of his men perished. His ships were not found for over 150 years. McClintock's expedition solved the fate of Franklin himself, but left unanswered many other questions about the expedition. The Franklin mystery continues to consume the passions of many Arctic historians and adventurers. They want to know what happened to the ships, where (if at all) the expedition's records were cached, why and where all the men died. A century and a half later, government-backed and private researchers head annually

In Those Days

to the central Canadian Arctic in search of the rest of the story of this incredibly inept but "pious, diffident, gentle" man.

In the late autumn of 1923, before the ice formed, Knud Rasmussen, on his expedition across Arctic North America, travelled with white trapper Peter Norberg and an Inuk named Qaqortingneq to Qavdlunaarsiorfik on the east coast of Adelaide Peninsula. There they found exactly what Qaqortingneq had told them to expect: sun-bleached bones of members of the long-lost Franklin expedition, as well as some pieces of cloth and leather. Rasmussen claimed that he was the first outsider to visit the spot. He gathered the bones, built a cairn over them, and raised two flags at half mast, the British and the Danish, giving the lost explorers their last honours. Respectfully, he wrote, "The deep footprints of tired men had once ended in the soft snow here by the low, sandy spit, far from home, from countrymen."

Here are two brief accounts that Rasmussen collected about meetings seven decades earlier between Nattilingmiut and men of the Franklin expedition, some struggling to survive, some already dead.

From Iggiaraarjuk, he collected this brief story:

My father Mangaq was with Tetgatsaq and Qablut on a seal hunt on the west side of King William's Land when they heard shouts, and discovered three white men who stood on shore waving to them. This was in spring; there was already open water along the land, and it was not possible to get in to them before low tide. The white men were very thin, hollow-cheeked, and looked ill. They were dressed in white man's clothes, had no dogs and were travelling with sledges which they drew themselves. They bought seal meat and blubber, and paid with a knife. There was great joy on both sides at this bargain, and the white men cooked the meat at once with the aid of the blubber, and ate it.

Later on the strangers went along to my father's tent camp and stayed there the night, before returning to their own little tent, which was not of animal skins but of something that was white like snow. At that time there were already caribou on King William's Land, but the strangers only seemed to hunt wildfowl; in particular there were many eider ducks and ptarmigan then. The earth was not yet alive and the swans had not come to the country.

Father and his people would willingly have helped the white men, but could not understand them. They tried to explain themselves by signs, and in fact learned to know a lot by this means. They had once been many, they said; now they were only few, and they had left their ship out in the pack-ice. They pointed to the south, and it was understood that they wanted to go home overland. They were not met again, and no one knows where they went to.[14]

And from Qaqortingneq himself, this one:

Two brothers were once out sealing northwest of Qeqertaq (King William Island). It was in spring, at the time when the snow melts away round the breathing holes of the seals. Far out on the ice they saw something black, a large black mass that could be no animal.

---

[14] Knud Rasmusen, *The Netsilik Eskimos: Social Life and Spiritual Culture. Report of the Fifth Thule Expedition 1921–24*, Vol. VIII, No. 1 (Copenhagen: Gyldendalske Boghandel, 1931), 129.

In Those Days

They looked more closely and found that it was a great ship. They ran home at once and told their fellow-villagers of it, and the next day they all went out to it. They saw nobody, the ship was deserted, and so they made up their minds to plunder it of everything they could get hold of. But none of them had ever met white men, and they had no idea what all the things they saw could be used for.

One man, who saw a boat hanging up over the gunwale, shouted: "A trough. A gigantic trough! I am going to have that!" He had never seen a boat and so he thought it was a meat trough. He cut through the lines that held the boat, and it crashed down on to the ice bottom upward and was smashed.

They found guns in the ship too, and as they had no suspicion of what they were, they knocked the steel barrels off and hammered them out for harpoons. In fact, so ignorant were they about guns that they said a quantity of percussion caps they found were "little thimbles", and they really thought that among the white men there lived a dwarf people who could use them.

At first they dared not go down into the ship itself, but soon they became bolder and even ventured into the houses that were under the deck. There they found many dead men lying in their beds. At last they also risked going down into the enormous room in the middle of the ship. It was dark there. But soon they found tools and would make a hole in order to let light in. And the foolish people, not understanding white man's things, hewed a hole just on the water-line so that the water poured in and the ship sank. And it went to the bottom with all the valuable things, of which they barely rescued any.

The same year, well into spring, three men were on their way from King William's Land to Adelaide Peninsula to hunt for caribou calves. There they found a boat with the bodies of six men. In the boat were guns, knives, and some provisions, showing that they had perished of sickness.

There are several other places in our country where we still see bones of these white men. . . .

That is all I know about the "pelrartut" as we call the white men who once visited our country and who were lost without our forefathers being able to help them.[15]

---

[15] Ibid., 130–131.

"A Nice Steady Lad and a Favourite with his Tribe"

Albert One-Eye

The lives of Inuit who served on Arctic expeditions are poorly recorded. Often a name is noted, but the amount of detail that follows is maddeningly meagre. One such man was Albert One-Eye, an Inuk born about 1824 on the east coast of James Bay, the so-called Eastmain of the Hudson's Bay Company.

One of the small mysteries that surrounds Albert's short but eventful life is his very name. It was unusual, in those far-off days, for an Inuk to use a surname. And this was an evocative surname, conveying an image of a one-eyed man in the service of explorers. Yet, in anything written about him by the men he served, there is no reference to any physical handicap. One suspects that he had none, and that "One-Eye" was indeed a quasi-surname—he was probably the son of a man who had lost an eye.

Of Albert's early life, nothing is known. In the summer of 1842, when he was about eighteen, he was at Rupert House. We know this because Chief Trader Thomas Corcoran of the Hudson's Bay Company arrived there that summer en route to lower James Bay. He took notice of Albert and thought that the "Esquimaux Boy," as he called him, should see Moose Factory. This would indicate that young Albert had some abilities and that Corcoran thought he could be of use to the company. So, on August 2, Albert sailed in the sloop *Speedwell* for the company's main post in the region.

At Moose Factory, Albert entered into a contract with the company to work for them for seven years as an apprentice labourer. His salary would be eight pounds a year for the first two years, rising every two years to ten pounds, twelve pounds, and finally fifteen pounds. But his duties would not keep him at Moose Factory. The same year he was hired he travelled back to Rupert House with an Indian from the Eastmain—which would indicate that relations between Inuit and Indians were good on that coast at the time—and from there he travelled on to the company's post at Fort George, where he and another Inuk named Moses acted as interpreters. It is obvious from this that it was the young man's abilities in English that had brought him to the notice of the company's chief trader.

Albert worked in the Rupert River District until early 1848. By then his apprenticeship period was not quite ended, but he was needed elsewhere. The previous year the British Admiralty had sent an expedition, led by Sir John Richardson, to search the Arctic coast between the Mackenzie and Coppermine rivers for the missing Franklin expedition. The Admiralty had requested that Albert join the expedition as interpreter and assistant. Albert's abilities as an interpreter must have been widely known by then, but it was probably through the expedition's second-in-command, John Rae, that he was brought to the Admiralty's attention.

* * *

John Rae had been born near the windswept town of Stromness on the Atlantic coast of the Orkney Islands on the last day of September 1813. The family home, the Hall of Clestrain, bore the brunt of Atlantic storms—when I stood there on a February afternoon, I felt as cold as I'd ever felt in the Arctic—and so perhaps it is no surprise that John Rae eventually ended up in the far North.

But first there was the matter of an education. Rae had been born into a well-to-do family, so he studied in Edinburgh at the Royal College of Surgery and became a doctor in 1833.

As did so many young men from Orkney, John Rae joined the Hudson's Bay Company, and served initially as a ship's surgeon on the company's vessel, *Prince of Wales*. On his first voyage, ice prevented the ship from making its return from Hudson Bay to Scotland, and Rae wintered with the ship in James Bay. While there, the company offered him a five-year contract as "clerk and surgeon," and so he remained in Rupert's Land, based at Moose Factory. There he earned a reputation for his ability as a long-distance walker. On one occasion he walked 105 miles to Fort Albany in two days to treat a patient. Later, returning from an Arctic expedition, Rae walked from Fort Chipewyan to Minnesota—1,720 miles—in fifty-four days. "A long day's march on snowshoes," he once commented, "is about the finest exercise a man can take." Rae travelled light, as did the native people he learned from, and lived off the land whenever he could.

Governor George Simpson of the Hudson's Bay Company suggested that Rae go to the Arctic to survey the uncharted portions of the North American coastline. Rae accepted the suggestion, but first went to Toronto to study surveying.

In all, he made four expeditions to the Arctic. It was on the second one, his search for Franklin, that he requested the services of Albert One-Eye.

* * *

Albert had been a valuable and popular employee of the company at Fort George. John Spencer, the trader there, was "exceedingly sorry to part with him." He wrote that Albert was "a nice steady lad, and a favourite with his Tribe."

On March 12, 1848, Albert reached Moose Factory and left shortly thereafter for the far northwest, travelling by way of Michipicoten and Cumberland House. He would never see his homeland again.

From Cumberland House, John Rae wrote a letter on June 13, 1848, to Governor Simpson. In it he stated that they were taking no hunters with them to the Arctic coast, and would depend on Rae's own hunting ability "and the exertions of our Esquimaux Interpreter," whom he described as "a fine active lad," who would "no doubt prove to be a good deer hunter." The lad he was referring to was Albert One-Eye.

In Those Days

In August, Albert was with Richardson and Rae in the Mackenzie Delta, and, according to Richardson, had no great difficulty in understanding and making himself understood by the Inuit there. The explorer's narrative tells little about the interactions between Albert and the Inuit of the delta, but one anecdote is perhaps instructive about the delicate work of being an interpreter.

In answer to Richardson's questions about whether any white men had been seen in the area, one man told him that a party of white men were living on Richard's Island. He didn't know that Richardson had been there the previous day. Richardson instructed Albert to tell the man that he knew he was lying. "He received this retort with a smile," wrote Richardson, "and without the slightest discomposure, but did not repeat his assertion." Albert probably conveyed Richardson's doubts about the man's truthfulness with considerably more tact than the explorer himself recounted it in his memoirs, for the role of an interpreter among his fellow Inuit, especially those distant and unknown, required diplomacy and discretion.

Early the following year, writing from Fort Confidence, their winter quarters at the northeastern corner of Great Slave Lake, Rae informed Governor Simpson of his plans to reach the Coppermine River. The crew would include Albert, once again described as "a very fine lad" and "fit for any of the duties of a labourer."

The men who travelled as part of such an expedition, with its attendant dangers, received a salary much higher than Albert had ever earned at a Hudson's Bay Company post. His was a whopping thirty-five pounds per year. Still, he was the lowest paid of any of the crew, everyone else earning forty-two pounds and the steersman forty-five pounds.

The party left Fort Confidence on June 7. They reached the Arctic coast in early July, and Albert found no difficulty in communicating with the Inuit they met there. But ice prevented them from crossing to Victoria Island where, the Coppermine Inuit reported, there lived Inuit who had never seen white men before. The party returned to Bloody Fall, the site where Samuel Hearne claimed to have witnessed the massacre of Inuit almost eight decades earlier, and began to travel up the Coppermine River on their return journey to Fort Confidence. Then, on August 24, tragedy struck.

They had successfully manoeuvred their boat up the dangerous part of the rapids and reached an area where the current was strong but the river smooth. Rae thought it was safe to take a loaded boat up the river, with some of the men onshore tracking with a small line.

Wrote Rae: "When halfway up, some unaccountable panic seized the steersman, and he called on the trackers to slack the line, which was no sooner done sufficiently far, than he and the bowsman sprung on shore, and permitted the boat to sheer out into midstream [where] the line snapped, and the boat driving broadside to the current was soon upset."

John Rae and Albert ran down the bank of the river, expecting the boat to get caught in an eddy. The boat passed close to where Albert stood waiting, and he managed to hook it by the keel with an oar. Rae ran to help him and snatched a pole from the water and jammed it into a broken plank. He called to Albert to hold on with him. Either Albert didn't hear him, or he thought he would be of more assistance on the capsized boat. He sprung onto the bottom of the boat just before the current carried it towards the head of a little bay. Rae thought Albert was safe there, but in less than a minute he saw the boat come out of the protection of the bay, driven by the current, and sink gradually beneath the water.

The last John Rae saw of Albert was the young man attempting to leap from the boat to the rocks. But he missed his target and disappeared into the water, "nor did he rise again to the surface."

John Rae placed the blame for Albert's death solely on James Hope, the Cree steersman, whom he described as "a notorious thief and equally noted for falsehood."

In 1848, Rae had been promoted by the company to be in charge of the Mackenzie River District, with his headquarters at Fort Simpson. He was to take up this post as soon as his service with Richardson was at an end, and he had hoped to retain Albert there as an employee. Recognizing the young man's abilities, Rae noted that "he would be useful in the event of it becoming desirable to have any negotiations with the Esquimaux at the mouth of the McKenzie [sic]," and he hoped "to make him in every way a most useful man to the Company."

The tragedy ended these well-intentioned plans. "This melancholy accident has distressed me more than I can well express," wrote Rae. "Albert was liked by every-one, for his good temper, lively disposition and great activity in doing anything that was required of him. I had become much attached to the poor fellow."

Charles Dickens, John Rae, and the "Good Interpreter," William Ouligbuck

John Rae's final Arctic expedition is his most well-known. After wintering at Repulse Bay in the winter of 1853–54, he set off northward in the spring on a surveying and mapping trip. From Inuit he heard reports of a large group of white men who had been in the area four years earlier, some dead, some dying. This could only be the crew of the Franklin expedition. From the Inuit, Rae acquired items that proved incontrovertibly that that was the case.

He reported the situation tersely to Governor Simpson: "Information has been obtained and articles purchased from the natives, which places the fate of a portion, if not all of the then survivors of Sir John Franklin's miserable party beyond a doubt—a fate the most deplorable—death from starvation, after having had recourse to cannibalism as a means of prolonging life."

In 1854 Rae returned to England with news of the fate of at least some of the men of the lost expedition. He reported what he had learned from Inuit, who had heard the information second-hand from other Inuit who had seen the bodies of some of the white men.

The following passage in Rae's report attracted considerable attention: "Some of the bodies had been buried . . . ; some were in a tent or tents; others under the boat, which had been turned over to form a shelter; and several lay scattered about in different directions. . . . From the mutilated state of many of the corpses and the contents of the kettles, it is evident that our wretched countrymen had been driven to the last resource—cannibalism—as a means of prolonging existence."

In a letter to the *Times*, he added: "Some of the corpses had been sadly mutilated, and had been stripped by those who had the misery to survive them, and who were found wrapped in two or three suits of clothes."

Although the British public, and Lady Franklin in particular, were horrified at the thought that British officers and seamen would resort to cannibalism, Rae nonetheless received the reward that had been offered to whoever would discover the fate of

Franklin. That reward was ten thousand pounds, and Rae shared it with the men he had travelled with on that expedition.

Charles Dickens was one of England's best-known and most-respected novelists of the mid–nineteenth century. His works are still widely read and studied in schools throughout the English-speaking world. But he didn't think much of Inuit. At the time of Rae's return, he was editor of a periodical called *Household Words*, and he took immediate objection to the suggestion that Englishmen would resort to cannibalism. He wrote, "It is in the highest degree improbable that such men as the officers and crews of the two lost ships would, or could, in any extremity of hunger, alleviate the pains of starvation by this horrible means."

Dickens thought that the Inuit reports Rae had conveyed to the British authorities and the public showed only the "loose and unreliable nature of the Esquimaux representations (on which it would be necessary to receive with great caution, even the commonest and most natural occurrence)." He referred again to the "improbabilities and incoherencies of the Esquimaux evidence." All this from a man who had never met an Inuk and never set foot in the Arctic. From the comfort of his desk in London, he challenged the reliability of the interpreter whom Rae used, claiming, on the basis of no evidence at all, that he was "in all probability, imperfectly acquainted with the language he translated to the white man."

Dickens claimed that "ninety-nine interpreters out of a hundred, whether savage, half-savage, or wholly civilised, interpreting to a person of superior station and attainments, will be under a strong temptation to exaggerate. This temptation will always be strongest, precisely where the person interpreted to is seen to be the most excited and impressed by what he hears;

for, in proportion as he is moved, the interpreter's importance is increased."

Gestures also played a part in the information the Inuit communicated to Rae, and Dickens seized on that information. "The gesture described to us as often repeated—that of the informant setting his mouth to his own arm," he wrote, "would quite as well describe a man having opened one of his veins, and drunk of the stream that flowed from it." He considered also the possibility that the bodies had been mutilated by bears or foxes, even by the ravages of scurvy, anything but the possibility that good and proper Englishmen would resort to "the last resource"—the euphemism often employed for cannibalism.

Finally Dickens considered the Inuit themselves:

"Lastly, no man can, with any show of reason, undertake to affirm that this sad remnant of Franklin's gallant band were not set upon by the Esquimaux themselves." "Savages," as Dickens considered the Inuit, were only respectful of white men when the white men were strong and in control. When they showed weakness, "the savage has changed and sprung upon him." He generalized about the character of those he considered "savages": "We believe every savage to be in his heart covetous, treacherous, and cruel; and we have yet to learn what knowledge the white man—lost, houseless, shipless, apparently forgotten by his race, plainly famine-stricken, weak, frozen, helpless, and dying—has of the gentleness of Esquimaux nature."

Dickens went on to analyze a number of cases where English explorers and adventurers had endured incredible hardship without resorting to cannibalism. He felt that "the vague babble of savages" John Rae had reported should not be used to impugn the integrity of British officers and men. Dickens was wrong, of course, and in a subsequent issue of *Household Words*, John Rae himself wrote to defend the Inuit among whom he had travelled and whose words he had faithfully reported.

* * *

Rae refuted Dickens's suggestion that the Inuit had murdered Franklin's men because they realized they were in a weakened condition or outnumbered, and therefore vulnerable. He related his own personal experience among the Inuit:

> In eighteen hundred and forty-six-seven I and a party of twelve persons wintered at Repulse Bay. In the spring my men were divided and scattered in all directions; yet no violence was offered, although we were surrounded by native families, among whom there were at least thirty men. By murdering us they would have put themselves in possession of boats and a quantity of cutlery of great value to them. . . . Last spring, I, with seven men, was almost in constant communication with a party four times our number. The savages made no attempt to harm us. Yet wood, saws, daggers, and knives were extremely scarce with them, and by getting possession of our boat, its masts and oars, and the remainder of our property, they would have been independent for years.[16]

Rae pointed out that the Inuit of Repulse Bay were not on friendly terms with their neighbours to the west, from whom the

---

[16] John Rae, "The Lost Arctic Voyagers," in Charles Dickens (ed.), *Household Words* (X.19, Whole Number 248, 1855): 434.

second-hand reports of the fate of Franklin's men had come. In fact, on occasion they had urged Rae to shoot several visitors from Pelly Bay, which, of course, Rae had refused to do. If the Inuit who initially reported the death of Franklin's men had murdered them, would not the Inuit whom Rae visited have reported that to him, in the hope that the Scotsman might take some revenge upon them?

No, the Inuit had told Rae the truth. And he asked, rhetorically, "Again, what possible motive could the Esquimaux have for inventing such an awful tale as that which appeared in my report to the secretary of the Admiralty?" He explained: "Alas! These poor people know too well what starvation is, in its utmost extremes, to be mistaken on such a point." The Inuit, he wrote, "resort to the 'last resource' only when driven to it by the most dire necessity. They will starve for days before they will even sacrifice their dogs to satisfy the cravings of their appetites."

Rae felt that Inuit were not above lying when they had something to gain from it—a pretty universal trait—but that "they cannot lie like truth, as civilised men do. Their fabrications are so silly and ridiculous, and it is so easy to make them contradict themselves by a slight cross-questioning, that the falsehood is easily discovered."

Overall he considered the Inuit to be "dutiful sons and daughters, kind brothers and sisters, and most affectionate parents." Moreover, he felt that most of those who interacted with the Inuit, whether they be Hudson's Bay Company employees like himself or missionaries, shared the same high opinion. This was a way of putting down Dickens, whom he acknowledged as "a writer of great ability and practice," for it was obvious that Dickens had never met an Inuk.

In concluding his lengthy letter to *Household Words*, John Rae was unwavering in his defence of the Inuit story:

> That my opinions remain exactly the same as they were when my report to the Admiralty was written, may be inferred from all I have now stated.
>
> That twenty or twenty-five Esquimaux could, for two months together, continue to repeat the same story without variation in any material point, and adhere firmly to it, in spite of all sorts of cross questioning, is to me the clearest proof that the information they gave me was founded on fact.
>
> That the "white men" were not murdered by the natives, but that they died of starvation is, to my mind, equally beyond a doubt.[17]

Dickens remained unconvinced. Ironically, when he was buried in the Poets' Corner of Westminster Abbey, the inscription on his tomb read in part: "He was a sympathiser to the poor, the suffering, and the oppressed." But his sympathies definitely did not lie with the Inuit.

* * *

What incensed John Rae the most were the aspersions cast on the abilities and integrity of his interpreter, William Ouligbuck, on whom he had relied heavily.

William Ouligbuck was born in Ungava Bay while his father, known simply as Ouligbuck, was employed there by the Hudson's

---

[17] John Rae, "The Lost Arctic Voyagers," in Charles Dickens (ed.), *Household Words* (X.20, 1855): 459.

In Those Days

Bay Company. Ouligbuck the elder eventually transferred back to Churchill, and his son spent most of his youth there and farther south at York Factory. His was a family with roots in the Kivalliq region, probably in the area of present-day Arviat, but that travelled widely throughout the Arctic. At some point the family, including young William, even lived far to the west in Fort Simpson while the elder Ouligbuck served the company.

The date of his birth is unrecorded, but it was sometime around 1831, for he was probably the boy referred to in 1843 by Letitia Hargrave, wife of a Hudson's Bay Company employee, as being a little scamp about twelve years of age who spoke ten languages. Although the lad went on to become a capable interpreter, surely this is an overstatement of his linguistic abilities.

While still a teenager, young Ouligbuck accompanied his father on John Rae's expedition of 1846–47. Mischievous teens were a reality in the 1840s as much as they are today, and Rae described him as an "incorrigible thief." Later, in 1853, while preparing for a surveying expedition that doubled as a search for the men of the missing Franklin expedition, Rae again needed an interpreter. Ouligbuck the father had died the previous year, and Rae said he would prefer not to employ the son, whom he considered "one of the greatest rascals unhung." But Inuit who could interpret in English were not in abundance a century and a half ago, so Rae reluctantly hired William Ouligbuck.

In one of his reports, Rae wrote that William Ouligbuck was prone to bouts of sulkiness, that he lied when it suited him, and that he was not particularly honest. But he also described him as a good interpreter, and this was the quality that Rae was looking for. At the end of the expedition, when Rae landed Ouligbuck at Churchill, he referred to him simply as his "good interpreter Wm. Ouligbuck."

Perhaps the young man had matured during the expedition. One thing is certain. Once Rae was back in England, he would brook no criticism of his interpreter. He defended him at length in his letter to Dickens's magazine, *Household Words*.

"William Ouligbuck speaks English fluently," he wrote, "and, perhaps, more correctly than one half of the lower classes in England and Scotland." He continued:

> As I could not, from my ignorance of the Esquimaux tongue, test William Ouligbuck's qualifications, I resorted to the only means of doing so I possessed. There is an old servant of the company at Churchill, an honest trustworthy man, who has acquired a very fair knowledge of both the Esquimaux character and the Esquimaux language. This man informed me that young Ouligbuck could be perfectly relied on; that he would tell the Esquimaux exactly what was said, and give the Esquimaux reply with equal correctness; that when he had any personal object to gain, he would not scruple to tell a falsehood to attain it, but in such a case the untruth was easily discovered by a little cross-questioning. This description I found perfectly true.[18]

Rae went on the state that there was little possibility of William Ouligbuck misunderstanding the dialect of the Inuit he had questioned, for "the natives of Repulse Bay speak precisely the same language as those of Churchill, where young Ouligbuck was brought up."

---

[18] Ibid., 433

In Those Days

Dickens had stated that interpreters were prone to exaggeration, especially if they perceived the possibility of reward. Not so, said Rae, who concluded his defence with this assertion: "That ninety-nine out of a hundred interpreters are under a strong temptation to exaggerate may be true. If so, my interpreter is the exception, as he did not like to talk more than he could possibly help. No doubt had I offered him a premium for using his tongue freely he might have done so; but not even the shadow of a hope of a reward was held out."

William Ouligbuck was paid at the rate of twenty British pounds per year for his assistance to Rae. Later, he received an unexpected bonus for his work. The Admiralty awarded Rae an eight-thousand-pound reward for ascertaining the fate of Franklin's expedition and an additional two thousand pounds to be divided among his men. Ouligbuck's share of the reward was 210 pounds, a fabulous bonus equal to ten years' salary.

William Ouligbuck worked sporadically for the Hudson's Bay Company at Churchill in subsequent years, for he was able to interpret in Inuktitut, English, Cree, and Chipewyan. Periodically he left to live the traditional life of a hunter, but always he returned. He retired from company service on June 1, 1894, and died sometime during the winter of 1895–96.

For John Rae, the years of trekking through the Arctic were over. He practiced medicine in Toronto and married there. The marriage was childless. He and his wife returned to Orkney and then, two years later, retired finally to London, where he died in 1893, at the age of seventy-nine. He was buried in the churchyard of St. Magnus Cathedral in Kirkwall in Orkney. Inside the cathedral a stunning memorial carved in stone was later erected, depicting Rae asleep on the tundra, still wearing his Arctic clothing, his gun by his side, a blanket tossed over him.

A biographer, C. Stuart Houston, has summed up Rae's character thus: "He was intelligent, an accurate observer, a competent writer, and an accomplished doctor. He was pleasant, cheerful, generous, and sensitive. He was frugal, conducting his surveys more economically than anyone before or since. He was sympathetic to the natives and willing to learn their methods of travel, hunting, and building snow houses. And he was candidly honest."

John Rae was a competent Arctic traveller, capable of making his own way on the land and hunting for his own survival. Nonetheless, whenever possible, he travelled with Indigenous people. In the Arctic he relied heavily on two Inuit men in particular: Albert One-Eye and William Ouligbuck. But sadly, there is no physical memorial anywhere to either man.

Inuit Evidence in a British Court

John Franklin and the crews of his ships *Erebus* and *Terror* left England in 1845 on the most famous expedition in Arctic history. They never returned.

On the fifteenth of May, 1845, only five days before the ships departed England, the mate of the *Erebus*, Lieutenant Edward Couch, made his will. In the event of his death, his estate was to go to his father, Captain James Couch.

No one knows when or precisely where the unfortunate Edward Couch died. He drew his last breath somewhere in the Canadian Arctic. But back home in England, four and a half years after he bid his son farewell, James Couch passed away in January 1850.

In 1854 the executor of Edward Couch's estate, a Mr. Ommaney, obtained probate of his will. The esoteric question the court had to decide was this: Had the father, James Couch, survived his son? Or had the son, Edward Couch, predeceased the father somewhere in the vastness of the Canadian Arctic? The court had to decide a question of survivorship: Who had died first?

Strangely enough, information provided indirectly by Canadian Inuit to John Rae was crucial in the court's difficult decision. And the Inuk William Ouligbuck was the conduit for the transfer of that information from the Inuit to the waiting ears and pen of John Rae.

An affidavit of the Arctic explorer was presented as the sole evidence in court. But although he stated clearly that the information came from Inuit, he did not credit William Ouligbuck by name as his source. Rae wrote:

> I arrived at Repulse Bay, in the Arctic Regions, in the month of August, 1853, and while engaged on such last-mentioned expedition, I, in the Spring and Summer of the year 1854, met with a party of the Esquimaux Tribe, who had in their possession and from whom I purchased and brought with me to this country, on my return thereto in the month of October, 1854, various articles which have . . . been identified . . . as belonging to or as having belonged to the said Sir John Franklin and some of the officers under him.[19]

Rae's affidavit went on to explain that he had obtained information from the Inuit he met in 1854 that in the spring of 1850, another

---

[19] John Rae, in *Ommanney v. Stilwell* (23 Beav 328) 53 ER 129, High Court of England, 1856; quoted in *The English Reports*, Vol. LIII, Rolls Court VI (Edinburgh: William Green & Sons, 1905), 129.

party of Inuit hunting near King William Island had encountered a party of about forty white men travelling southward over the ice, dragging a boat and sledges with them. The white men could not speak Inuktitut, but through signs had communicated to the Inuit that their ships had been crushed by ice. The men, who could only have been from Sir John Franklin's expedition, were thin and short of provisions, and obtained some seal meat from the Inuit. Later that spring, the same group of Inuit discovered on the mainland of North America the bodies of about thirty white men and some graves, and five more dead bodies on a nearby island. Rae's affidavit stated that "some at least of such white men must have survived until the arrival of wild fowl at the said places where such dead bodies were found, as the reports of the firing off of guns were heard by such party of other Esquimaux people, and the fresh bones and feathers of wild geese were noticed by them to be there."

Rae knew from his experience that wild geese would not reach the region until late May or early June. He continued: "the fresh bones and feathers of such geese, mentioned, by the said Esquimauxs [sic], as having been seen where such dead bodies were said to have been found . . . lead me to conclude, that some of the white men survived until at least the latter end of the month of May or the beginning of the month of June, in the year 1850."

So some of the white men of Franklin's doomed party had survived until late spring of 1850. The question was: Was Edward Couch among those survivors?

On the answer to that question hung the fate of the estate of Edward Couch. The Court was faced with the impossible question of determining whether he was among the white men who had survived in the Arctic until the late spring of 1850, in which case Edward Couch would have survived his father.

Why did it matter?

If Edward was deemed to have died first, his estate would pass to his father, whose estate (now including the value of his son's estate) would pass to the father's other heirs on his death. But if Edward was deemed to have survived his father, the father's estate would pass to his designated beneficiaries, which included Edward, and Edward's estate would pass, through common law, to his next of kin. Those next of kin—who included a man named William Couch—may not have been the same as the individuals who would have inherited James's (the father's) estate. So money was at stake.

Lawyers for William Couch, described only as "one of the next of kin of Edward at his death," argued that under British law, Edward could not be presumed dead until seven years had passed since he had last been known to have been alive, and since his father had died less than five years after Edward was last known to be alive, the Court must conclude that Edward survived his father, in which case William would stand to inherit some money. Thomas Stilwell, executor of the father's, James Couch's, estate, argued the opposite position.

The case went to Chancery Court for argument. This was a division of the Court that decided points of law on the basis of fairness, rather than a mere application of the law.

The Master of the Rolls, the third most senior judge of England and Wales, was Sir John Romilly, and he had to make the difficult decision. Of course, he had no way of knowing when Edward Couch had died, any more than any of the others involved in the matter. It came down to a question of probability:

In Those Days

This case involves a question of as great difficulty as any I have ever had to deal with; not only from the want of evidence, but from the tendency of the evidence which exists to create doubt.

The sole question is, whether the son or the father died first. The father died in January, 1850, and the son, who was an active, strong young man, went as mate with Sir John Franklin in 1845, and the question is whether he died before January, 1850. That is the sole question.

The ordinary presumption that a person who has not been heard of for seven years would apply, if there were nothing else on the subject.[20]

But there was something else on the subject. And that was Inuit evidence, collected by John Rae. The Master, however, in continuing his judgment, ignored the Inuit and incorrectly attributed everything to Rae:

The evidence which exists is that of Dr. Rae. He discovered the remains of various persons who had perished from hunger belonging to the expedition of Sir John Franklin. It is clear that the persons who were seen in April survived the father; they were about forty in number, while the original number was 133, and no identity is proved.

In this state of things, I confess I cannot come to a satisfactory conclusion on the subject. My Chief Clerk is of opinion that the son survived the father, and has made or was about to make a certificate accordingly. He relied on

---

[20] Ibid., 130.

the youth and strength of the son. I cannot see that this conclusion is erroneous. I cannot but express my extreme inability to come to a satisfactory conclusion, but relying on the chances in favour of the youth and strength of the son, I see no reason to differ from the conclusion of the Chief Clerk.[21]

So William Couch benefited from the estate of his unfortunate relative, Edward. He owed his good fortune to Inuit oral evidence provided second-hand through William Ouligbuck to a persistent Arctic explorer.

---

[21] Ibid.

A Fortuitous Meeting

Tookoolito and Ipiirvik, and Charles Francis Hall

"Good morning, sir."

The voice was feminine, the tone musical and lively. The language was English, and the impression was of a lady of refinement.

Charles Francis Hall, neophyte Arctic explorer, looked up from his desk, where he was recording the events of November 2, 1860. He had not expected to hear a female voice aboard the whaler *George Henry*, anchored in Cyrus Field Bay off the coast of Baffin Island. "The tone," he wrote, "instantly told me that a lady of refinement was there, greeting me. I was astonished. Could I be dreaming? Was it a mistake? No! I was wide awake and writing. But, had a thunder-clap sounded on my ear, though it was snowing at the time, I could not have been more surprised than I was at the sound of that voice."

Even less was he expecting what he saw as he trained his eyes toward the source of this pleasing sound. A flood of light from a skylight in the main cabin silhouetted his visitor in the doorway. He could make out a shadowy figure in a multicultural costume: a dress with heavy flounces, a jacket of caribou fur, and a "kiss-me-quick" bonnet. At first he could not make out her features, but he soon discerned that the lady was Inuit. She extended an ungloved hand to Hall. "Whence," thought the explorer, "came this civilization refinement?"

She entered the cabin at his invitation. And then he realized. This was Tookoolito, whom the whalers called Hannah and spoke of with such respect. He had, in fact, been hoping to meet her. Her husband followed her into the cabin. His name was Ipiirvik—though Hall spelled it Ebierbing—but the whalers knew him as Joe, a skilled ship's pilot often in the employ of whaling masters.

Tookoolito, Hall noted, "spoke my own language fluently." Ipiirvik—whom Hall described as "a fine, and also intelligent-looking man"—did not speak English as well as his wife, yet Hall was able to talk with him "tolerably well." They told the explorer about their visit to England seven years earlier, recounting that they had dined with Prince Albert—a "very kind, good man," Ipiirvik said. He described Queen Victoria as "quite pretty." Tookoolito said of the queen, "I visited her, and liked the appearance of her majesty, and every thing about the palace. Fine place, I assure you, sir."

In Those Days

Hall talked at length with Tookoolito. He recorded his first impressions thus: "I could not help admiring the exceeding gracefulness and modesty of her demeanour. Simple and gentle in her way, there was a degree of calm intellectual power about her that more and more astonished me."

Hall realized, of course, that this Inuit couple could be of great assistance to him in his efforts to learn the fate of the lost Franklin expedition, the mission that had brought him north on this shoestring expedition and which would drive him for the next decade. He took the couple on as his interpreters and guides. Two weeks later he wrote, "I feel greater confidence . . . in the success of my mission since engaging these two natives. They can talk with me in my own vernacular, are both smart, and will be useful each in the department they will be called upon to fill."

On his first meeting with them, aboard the *George Henry*, Hall asked Tookoolito if she would like to live in England again. She replied courteously, "I would like very well, I thank you." Then he got right to the point. "Would you like to go to America with me?" he asked. "Indeed I would, sir," came the ready reply.

Hall noted in his journal for that day: "I felt delighted beyond measure, because of the opportunity it gave me for becoming better acquainted with these people through her means, and I hoped to improve it toward the furtherance of the great object I had in view."

This brief but auspicious visit would forever change the lives of Tookoolito and Ipiirvik. In 1862 they would travel to America with Hall, then, a few years later, accompany him on a five-year journey to Hudson Bay and the central Canadian Arctic in search of the remains of the lost Franklin expedition. In between expeditions, they lived in a two-storey frame house that they purchased on the outskirts of Groton, Connecticut. Later they would be part of the ill-fated *Polaris* expedition, and survive the amazing drift of nineteen people on an ice floe from northern Greenland to the North Atlantic. They became the most well-travelled Inuit of their time.

* * *

But Tookoolito and Ipiirvik paid a high price for their free trip to America. On their voyage with Hall, they were accompanied by their first child, a boy called Tarralikitaq. The name meant "butterfly." Hall usually wrote it Tuk-e-lik-e-ta, and said, "I never saw a more animated, sweet-tempered, bright-looking child. Its imitativeness was largely developed, and was most engaging. Tuk-e-lik-e-ta was a child to be remembered by all who ever saw him." After a time in America, he was simply called Johnny.

Hall had offered the Inuit couple an opportunity to visit America, but he had mentioned nothing about exhibitions. Nonetheless, Tookoolito and Ipiirvik probably expected that they would be put on display—after all, they had been extensively exhibited for profit and publicity when they were in England. Why should America be different? Promoters were in the habit of recruiting people of different ethnic backgrounds and presenting them in carnivals, circuses, or lectures. But it would not be the Inuit who benefited from these exhibitions, but Hall, financially and in terms of publicity to raise his profile for his next polar venture.

Hall wasted no time. On the week commencing Monday, November 3, they were exhibited at Barnum's Museum "every day and evening." They were advertised as the "Esquimaux Family, Just brought to this country, From Davis Straits, Greenland." The geography was wrong, of course. The poster advertising their exhibition went on to say that "the notoriety recently given to this singular race of men by the several Arctic exploring expeditions, including Dr. Kane's, Dr. Hays [sic], and Mr. Hall's, has invested them with an interest in the public mind, which no other race at the present time possesses." They were displayed three times daily, from 10 a.m. to 12 noon, from 2 to 4 in the afternoon, and from 7 to 10 in the evening. The price of admission was twenty-five cents. Tookoolito, Ipiirvik, and their baby appeared with human side-show attractions, performing bears, and a family of albinos.

By January 1863, Ipiirvik was sick. In a letter to his wealthy benefactor, Henry Grinnell, Hall wrote: "Returned from Eskimo yesterday noon. Owing to the severe illness of Ebierbing, the man Esquimaux, could not call till now. Ebierbing took a cold while at Elmira. Was up with him nearly all last night—hope to be able to report more favorably of him to-morrow. As the Esquimaux desire to remain with me, have taken a [suite?] of rooms at a low price that will accommodate them and myself."

Indeed, the record of the time these Inuit spent in the United States reads like a litany of illnesses. They had no immunity to the diseases that were common outside the Arctic, and, like other Inuit who travelled to America or Europe before and after them, they were prone to colds, flu, and tuberculosis.

Sidney O. Budington, the ship's captain who had brought Hall and his party to America, objected to Hall's exploitation of the family. He thought their health was beginning to show the strains of the constant activity. Finally Hall wrote to Budington, asking if he and his wife would once again care for the family. But even before arrangements for their transportation to Groton could be made, Tarralikitaq died in New York on February 28. He was only eighteen months old.

Hall wrote that both parents felt the loss of their infant son greatly, "but to the mother it was a terrible blow. For several days after its death she was unconscious, and for a part of the time delirious. When she began to recover from this state she expressed a longing desire to die, and be with her lost Tuk-e-lik-e-ta."

The Budingtons attended to the funeral of Tarralikitaq. He was buried in the Starr Burying Ground, not far from the Budington family plot, on the outskirts of Groton. More than a decade later, his mother would join him there.

* * *

Charles Francis Hall had a conflicted relationship with the Inuit couple. Although he unashamedly exploited them and was in some measure responsible for the death of their son, at the same time he had a genuine affection for them. And it is to Hall that we owe our gratitude that their names appear on the map of Northern Canada.

Hall liberally sprinkled new place names, English and Inuktitut, wherever he travelled, oblivious to the fact that many of the places had perfectly good Inuktitut names already.

The Inuktitut names of the couple in question appear among the names in the jumble of islands, bays, and promontories that clutter the waters off Hall Peninsula, the promontory separating Frobisher Bay from Cumberland Sound. And so we find Tookoolito Inlet at 63°05' north latitude and 64°45' west longitude. Nearby we find Ebierbing Bay at 63°14' north and 64°55' west. These remain, thankfully, the official place names of these locations.

It should be noted that on the map that accompanied the publication of Hall's first book in 1864, the names were spelled differently. Tookoolito's name was spelled Too-hoo-li-to (Hall generally spelled Inuktitut names in syllables separated by hyphens), and Ipiirvik (Ebierbing) was rendered as E-bien-bing. Although Hall was atrocious at spelling Inuktitut names, he wasn't usually this bad, and he did spell their names differently in the text of his book. I'd like to suggest that the strange spellings on the map should be attributed to the challenges the map's lithographer, J. Schedler of New York, had in understanding Hall's difficult handwriting.

In Greenland, we must look very far to the north to find the names of the famous couple. And they are commemorated differently than they are in Canada. Whereas in Canada both names are affixed to bodies of water and labelled in Inuktitut, in Greenland they are both remembered by their English names, which refer to tiny islands.

Joe Island is a few miles north of Cape Morton, off the tip of Petermann Peninsula, at 81°12' north, 63°28' west. It has been described simply as "a mushroom-shaped islet several hundred feet high."

Hannah Island is a little to the south, lying in the mouth of Bessels Bay. It is 120 feet high and was described simply as an immense heap of pebbles and drift that appeared to be the terminal moraine of a large glacier, now extinct.

It is doubtful if either of these islands had a native name in historic times, for it is doubtful if Inuit—in this case the Inughuit of northwestern Greenland—travelled that far north in the years before they were routinely recruited by American and British expeditions as guides and assistants. It's not certain who gave Hannah and Joe islands their names, but it may well have been Emil Bessels, scientist on Hall's *Polaris* expedition. Had it been

Hall, before his death, he probably would have used their Inuktitut names. Ironically, Bessels is the chief suspect in the death by poisoning of Hall.

Joe and Hannah were adopted as the official names of both islands by the Danish Committee on Geographical Naming on April 29, 1957, but of course the English word for "island" was replaced by the Danish word, the single-letter "Ø." So today they are officially Joe Ø and Hannah Ø.

In August 1875 Captain George Nares of the British ship *Alert*, accompanied by Commander Albert Hastings Markham, climbed to the top of Hannah Island and erected a cairn. In 1905 Robert Peary's ship *Roosevelt*, made fast to the ice foot on Joe Island, and Peary climbed to the island's summit to survey ice conditions ahead. Other than these few references, Hannah and Joe islands go generally unremarked in the record of Northern history. But they are there, as permanent reminders on the Northern map of the presence and heroism of this most amazing Inuit couple.

Another of the names that Charles Francis Hall placed on the map of Baffin Island, Tukeliketa Bay, north of Cyrus Field Bay, commemorated Tookoolito and Ipiirvik's young son, who died in New York in 1863.

Unfortunately, neither the child nor his name on the map survived. The name on the map disappeared in 1944 when the United States Hydrographic Service asked the Canadian Department of Mines and Resources, Surveys and Engineering Branch, to confirm as official a list of 247 names in Frobisher Bay and vicinity for a marine map the US government was making. One of the names on the list was Tukelik Bay. Somehow, over the years, Hall's Tukeliketa had been abbreviated to Tukelik.

In Those Days

K. G. Chipman, a member of the Executive Committee of the Geographic Board of Canada, was not satisfied with the spelling of five of the Inuktitut place names listed, and wanted the "form and spelling" referred to the anthropologist Diamond Jenness, then an advisor to the board.

Jenness studied the list and commented that Tukelik was probably intended to be "Tarkalikitark, meaning butterfly or moth," noting that "the word cannot be shortened and still retain any meaning." Jenness was correct in that "Tarkalikitark" cannot be abbreviated. But ironically, he seemed unaware that "tukilik" (pronounced the same as the offending "tukelik") means, among other possibilities, "that which has meaning"! Jenness misunderstood or simply didn't know the meanings of some of the other Inuktitut words on Chipman's list and recommended that some be replaced with English names.

When Chipman saw Jenness's reply, he wrote back to J. H. Corry, the board's secretary, with his opinion: "I think it would simply make the Board appear ridiculous if we were to approve Eskimo names which are meaningless and unintelligible or inexplicable. I recommend that the advice of Dr. Jenness be followed."

Inexplicably, F. H. Peters, the surveyor-general and chief of the Hydrographic Service, instead of using Jenness's spelling of Tarkalikitark or restoring the original Tukelikita to the map in place of the discredited Tukelik, recommended it be discarded completely and replaced with the English translation Butterfly Bay. None of the other four Inuktitut names that Chipman had questioned survived Jenness's and Peters's scrutiny either. One was replaced with an English mistranslation. The others were replaced with English names that had nothing to do with the original Inuktitut ones.

And so, through a series of errors and misunderstandings, the name of Tarralikitaq, son of Ipiirvik and Tookoolito, survives on the map of Baffin Island, only in translated form as Butterfly Bay.

Inuit Adrift

1,500 Miles on an Ice Floe

In 1872, Charles Francis Hall's exploration ship, the *Polaris*, broke free from its winter quarters at Thank God Harbor in northern Greenland. Hall had died—probably poisoned—the previous fall, and Sidney O. Budington, the captain, gave up any idea of trying to head farther north. At any rate, he had little control over where the ship went, for although it was out of the harbour, it was locked in drifting ice, moving slowly southward.

Then on October 15, a strong northern gale damaged the vessel. The captain decided, prematurely as it turned out, to abandon ship. The result was that some of the ship's complement remained aboard ship, while others ended up on an ice floe with a hodgepodge of provisions and equipment and no way to return to the vessel.

When the blizzard subsided, Captain George Tyson—he had been the *Polaris*'s ice-master—assessed the situation on the ice floe. Their floating prison was a nearly circular piece of ice, about four miles in circumference. Besides Tyson, there were eighteen people on the ice, including all of the expedition's Inuit. These were the famous Tookoolito and Ipiirvik, who had accompanied Hall on all his northern journeys, their daughter, and the Greenlander Hans Hendrik and his family. The Qallunaat, except Tyson, one other American, and an Englishman, were all Europeans, mostly German.

They did not see the *Polaris* again. Thus began one of the most amazing survival stories in the annals of Arctic history. Nineteen men, women, and children, adrift on an ice floe, survived for 196 days while their floe drifted slowly southward through Smith Sound, Baffin Bay, Davis Strait, and into the North Atlantic.

George Tyson became famous for his role on this unbelievable drift, for he kept a journal of the events that was turned into a best-selling book, *Arctic Experiences*, by a writer, E. Vale Blake. But it was the Inuit men, Ipiirvik and Hans Hendrik, who were the true heroes of the disaster, and who saved the entire group.

Tyson immediately instructed the Inuit to build three snow houses. He would live in one with Ipiirvik's family, Hans and his family would live in another, and the sailors would live in the third. Tyson wrote of his choice to live with Ipiirvik's family: "I prefer living with him, as both he and his wife, and even the child, can speak English, while in the men's hut I hear nothing but German, which I do not understand."

The sailors were quite helpless on the ice. Were it not for the presence of Ipiirvik and Hans, there is little doubt that the entire party would have perished. But in heeding Budington's call to abandon ship, both Inuit men had hastily thrown their kayaks onto the ice floe, along with paddles and other hunting equipment. Now their floating home formed a platform from which to launch their kayaks and hunt for the entire party. Often they returned empty-handed, but whenever they were successful, Tyson tried to ensure that everyone got their fair share of the food. As often as not, though, the Germans would appropriate everything for themselves. Often everyone was hungry.

On November 21, the ice-master wrote in his journal, "Puney [Panik, Hannah and Joe's daughter] is often hungry, indeed, all the children often cry with hunger. We give them all that is safe to use. I can do no more, however sorry I may feel for them." But it wasn't only the children who were hungry. Another of Tyson's journal entries notes, "Puney . . . sat looking at me for some time, and then gravely remarked, 'You are nothing but bone!' And, indeed, I am not much else."

In December, Ipiirvik began to fear that the German sailors were plotting to kill and eat the Inuit. He told Tyson that he didn't like the look in the men's eyes, and he voluntarily turned his pistol over to Tyson. "God forbid that any of this company should be tempted to such a crime!" Tyson wrote. "However, I have the pistol now, and it will go hard with any one who harms even the smallest child on this God-made raft."

Tyson had a deep respect for the Inuit, especially Ipiirvik. But there was a practicality to his approach, too. "Setting aside the crime of cannibalism," he continued, "it would be the worst possible policy to kill the poor natives. They are our best, and I may say only, hunters; no white man can catch seal like an Esquimau, who has practiced it all his life. It would be like 'killing the goose which lays the golden egg.' I shall protect the natives at all cost."

They drifted onward, slowly southward. At times they were quite close to the Baffin shore. At one point they drifted so close to the mouth of Cumberland Sound that Ipiirvik thought the Inuit could make it over the ice to shore near his own homeland. But he was a man of honour, even when his own life was endangered. He would not abandon Tyson and the others of the party.

In March their situation worsened. In a storm their floe disintegrated into smaller pieces, and they had to take to their small boat in heavy seas to find refuge on a larger piece of ice. That floe split in two, cutting through the middle of Ipiirvik's hastily constructed hut. By April they had passed the mouth of Hudson Strait and were adrift in the North Atlantic. As they entered warmer water, their small floe became increasingly fragile. They could not survive much longer.

On April 28, 1873, heavy waves made the remnants of their ice floe unsafe. They abandoned it and once again took to the ship's boat that they had taken when they had abandoned the *Polaris* six months earlier. That afternoon, from the unsteadiness of the storm-tossed boat, Ipiirvik shot three hooded seals, which he and Hans hauled into the boat.

Later that afternoon their hopes soared, only to plummet again, when they saw a steamer in the distance, a sealing vessel heading southwest. But the crew aboard the steamer didn't see them. George Tyson was nonetheless optimistic. There would be other ships. It was sealing season for Newfoundlanders, whose vessels would be plying the waters off Labrador. There might also be whalers. That evening they made camp on another small ice floe and burned seal blubber to attract any vessels that might be in the vicinity.

In Those Days

The next day they spotted another steamer. Everyone took to the boat again and the men rowed steadily for an hour in her direction. But although the sealer remained in sight for most of the day, and another one appeared late in the afternoon, the hapless ice-floe party remained invisible in the vastness of the North Atlantic.

On the last day of April, Tyson, catching a nap in the boat, was roused by the shouts of the watchman crying, "There's a steamer! There's a steamer!" A sealer had materialized through the heavy fog, not more than a quarter mile away. Tyson sprang to life, ordering all the guns to be fired and everyone to set up a simultaneous shout. At the same time, Hans took to his kayak and paddled furiously to intercept the vessel before it could once again disappear into the fog. This time, luck was with them. The steamer turned its bow in their direction.

But Hans paddled on, calling out in his broken English, "American steamer," by which words he meant to tell the sealers that the American steamer *Polaris* had been lost. The startled Newfoundlanders onboard gazed from their deck into the fog-shrouded waters, thunderstruck at seeing an Inuk in a kayak alongside. They took him aboard and, following his garbled instructions, steamed to the rescue of Tyson and the ice-bound party. Hans tried to tell them where they had come from, but the Newfoundlanders could not understand him. It didn't matter. In a few minutes, the sealer was alongside the tiny ice floe.

The vessel was the *Tigress* from Conception Bay, under Captain Isaac Bartlett. Tyson recounts his story of the rescue:

Two or three of their small seal-boats were instantly lowered. . . . The crews got on our bit of ice and peeped curiously into the dirty pans that we had used over the oil-fires.

124

We had been making soup out of the blood and entrails of the last seal which Hans had shot. They soon saw enough to convince them that we were in sore need. No words were required to make that plain.

Taking the women and children in their boats, we tumbled into our own, and were soon alongside of the *Tigress*. We left all we had behind, and our all was simply a few battered smoky tin pans and the debris of our last seal.

Thanks largely to the heroic hunting efforts of Ipiirvik and Hans and the leadership of George Tyson, this party of nineteen men, women, and children had drifted for over six months over a distance of fifteen hundred miles through some of the most treacherous waters in the world with no loss of life. It is one of mankind's greatest yet little-known stories of the will to live and of ultimate survival.

And it ends on a note of humour. On stepping aboard the *Tigress*, Tyson was surrounded by the curious sealers, all peppering him and his party with questions. "But," noted Tyson, "when they asked me, 'How long have you been on the ice?' and I answered 'Since the 15th of last October,' they were so astonished that they fairly looked blank with wonder."

Finally one of the sealers, staring at Tyson with "open-eyed surprise," blurted out a question:

"And was you on it night and day?"

For the first time in over six months, Tyson roared with laughter.

An Inuit Plan to Find the North Pole

S mith Sound is the body of water separating Ellesmere Island from Greenland at their closest points. It is the route that American and British explorers used in their attempts in the late 1800s to reach the North Pole. Those early attempts all ended in failure. Often the explorers returned with stories of how they had been on the verge of success. More money and another expedition were usually suggested as ways to solve the problems.

In 1876 the *New York Times* published a satirical article ridiculing these efforts:

The record of recent Arctic exploration is exceedingly monotonous. The expeditions of Kane, Hayes, Hall, and

Nares, successively started with well-equipped vessels, ostensibly to reach the North Pole. They stopped at Upernavik, in Greenland, long enough to send word home that they were in excellent spirits, and confident of success, and then proceeded up Smith's Sound, in order to get into winter quarters in the neighbourhood of the eightieth degree of latitude.

As to how the explorers passed their time while in winter quarters, we have, of course, only their own testimony, but we all know that not one of them ever reached the Pole. On the contrary, they uniformly returned at unexpected periods, with the report that on reaching eighty-two degrees of latitude . . . they found further progress impossible, and so returned home to mention the fact. . . .

It is impossible that this sort of thing should go indefinitely without invoking the suspicions of the long-suffering and credulous public. The time will come when people will insist upon knowing what is the attraction which makes most officers so anxious to go into winter quarters in Smith's Sound. Their pretence of wanting to go to the North Pole is altogether too transparent, and their excuses for returning home without having achieved their professed object are suspiciously contradictory.

Kane and Hayes asserted that they found an open polar sea, which they could not cross because they were unfortunately unprovided with the proper boats.

Hall said that instead of an open polar sea there was a nice overland road to the Pole, over which he promised to travel in sledges, but as he died before he was quite ready to return home, he avoided the task of explaining why his promised sledge journey was not undertaken.

In Those Days

As for Capt. Nares, he informs us that he did not go to the Pole because in so doing he would have been obliged to cross a frozen sea, where the ice was only 160 feet in thickness. What his precise weight is we are not told, but even if he weighs four hundred pounds, the ice was thick enough to bear him. The English people may not be very familiar with ice, but they cannot help knowing that ice 160 feet thick can be crossed, with reasonable care, by even the heaviest naval officer in the service. . . .

When four successive expeditions spend a winter in Smith's Sound, and return with the report that they could not reach the Pole because there was too much ice or too little ice, or because there was an open polar sea or because there was not an open polar sea, intelligent people cannot avoid the conclusion that there is something in this business which is kept from them, and will demand to know the true reason why explorers are so anxious to spend a winter in Smith's Sound.[22]

* * *

An anonymously authored newspaper article published in 1882 was way ahead of its time.

In that year, the Richwood, Ohio, *Reporter* published an article called simply "The Esquimaux." In it, the reporter heaped praise on Inuit for their accomplishments.

"Even the comparatively civilized inhabitants of Mexico never constructed arched vaults of stone as these Arctic dwellers have

---

[22] "The Arctic Mystery," *The New York Times* (October 30, 1876): 4.

done [of snow]," he wrote, adding that they used sleds long before other inhabitants of the Americas, and they used dogs to pull them when even the ancient Incas of Peru had never used animals in this way. And "they did this while they themselves were in the stone age."

Moreover, the Inuit were "inventive and highly ingenious," claimed the article, stating that no modern boat builder could compete with them in constructing light boats for rough water, and "no modern oarsman dreams of such feats in the management of boats as they constantly perform." Their fur dressing was unmatchable. They were mighty hunters, and "they invent weapons and means of making them from bones and ivory in a land where wood is often as rare as gold." They were skilled carvers and fashioned beautiful children's toys from ivory. They warmed their huts with seal-oil lamps. They made window lights of "fine transparent sealskin."

Moreover, they were "faithful and peaceable." The author noted the service of Inuit guides and map-makers to many Arctic explorers. In particular, he praised the work of the Greenlander Hans Hendrik and of Baffin Island's "Esquimau Joe," both of whom had been responsible for saving the lives of the sailors on the *Polaris* ice drift.

The writer obviously thought highly of the Inuit, but not of their homeland. It was barely possible, he claimed, for a white man—even with the help of Inuit—to live off the country, where "nature seems armed with all the horrors of one of the circles of Dante's hell." Too many lives of white men had been lost in Arctic exploration because the men were unfitted, physically, to cope with the hardships of an Arctic winter. Too much money had been spent in searches for the North Pole, and then in searches for the lost searchers. But the Inuit themselves existed in this Arctic desert and apparently thrived.

The writer then came up with a novel suggestion: to educate the Inuit, but only for the limited purpose of finding the North Pole. "There is no good reason," he claimed, "why we cannot safely undertake the education of at least enough Esquimaux to enable them to learn the objects of the quest for the Pole, the conditions under which science asserts the task can best be attempted, and what to look for when the goal is reached." This suggestion was made a century and a quarter before today's discussions of the interactions that should take place between Inuit traditional knowledge and science.

"These are the people to do the work," the writer proclaimed. "It is for us to show them how to do it."

He suggested the establishment of "some kind of school" to be located at an intermediate point where Inuit could live "without being rendered physically unfit for the resumption of their former mode of life in high latitudes," and where white men could also live without material discomfort. The next expedition north should encourage intelligent young men to relocate to this explorers' school, he suggested. Eventually, after learning why and how to find the North Pole, they should be returned north to their own people "and left to their own devices." The writer predicted that the expense of such an experiment might well be less than the cost of fitting out an expedition.

If his plan was implemented, the author thought, before long news would come out of the Arctic that the North Pole had been found, "and so, perhaps, in this way might be solved the problem which thus far has vanquished the energy and skill of the civilized world."

Of course, no school for Inuit explorers was ever established, and explorers continued for a few decades more to search for the elusive North Pole.

* * *

In early January of 1909, the Arctic Club of America met for its Fifteenth Annual Dinner at the Hotel Marlborough in New York. The club, a loose affiliation of men interested in the Arctic and its exploration, had been founded by those who had gone north in the summer of 1894 on Dr. Frederick Cook's disastrous *Miranda* expedition, an accident-ridden tourist voyage to Greenland. The club had grown in the fifteen years since its formation, and its members were all successful men.

Professor William Brewer and Admiral Winfield Schley, who in 1884 had commanded the party that had gone to the relief of the Greely expedition, spoke enthusiastically that night about the expedition they were planning to send out that summer in search of Dr. Cook. Cook had gone north in 1907 as a rival to Peary on his own search for the North Pole, and had not been heard of since.

A young Inuk was in attendance that night. Minik Wallace had been taken to New York by Robert Peary in 1897 and had remained in the city since then. He was by then in his late teens. Often invited to attend the club's meetings, he was sometimes asked to come dressed in his furs, a kind of living Arctic attraction.

Minik listened with rapt interest to the plans for the Cook relief expedition. It was no secret to members of the club that Minik was skeptical about white explorers' efforts to reach the top of the world, and that he had formulated some ideas of his own about the North Pole. Educated in New York, separated from his own people for a decade, he had read voraciously everything he could lay his hands on about the Arctic, and particularly the expeditions that had gone to his Arctic, northwestern Greenland, in search of the Pole. He had concluded that neither Cook nor Peary nor any other white explorer would ever reach the North Pole because their methods were all wrong.

But he had gone a step further. He had conceived a plan for an all-Inuit expedition to the Pole. His guardian, William Wallace, had once claimed, "Our object had been to educate him to be an explorer, for it had always been his theory and ours that if anyone reached the Pole it would be an Eskimo."

Minik explained his plan, with cutting sarcasm for the methods used by the most recent spate of Arctic explorers. His frankness, as reported in a newspaper article some time after the Arctic Club's dinner, must have made the club's members cringe with uneasiness.

"The explorers who are trying to find the North Pole now don't know how to do it," he claimed.

They fit out nice comfortable ships, take along a number of useless passengers to eat up their provisions and sail as far North as they can in one summer and passively wait until they are frozen in. Then they while away a winter eating up their provisions until summer comes again, when they make a so-called "dash," in which they sometimes cover as much as a mile a day, going as far as they can in half the summer. The other half of the summer is spent in beating it back to their ship before the Arctic winter becomes too severe. Then they return to the United States in a blaze of glory, announce that the pole is to be discovered "not yet, but soon," and start out on a long and profitable lecture tour, telling why they failed and how they will surely succeed next time.[23]

He explained:

"The North Pole will never be discovered in such a way. The man who finds it will go as far as he can in one season and make a permanent camp there until the next season. Then he will continue on his journey, and in such a way he must succeed. That's what I want to do. . . . I want to be the first man to find the Pole, so that the honor will go to one of my own race."

Minik returned north that summer, only to learn that both Cook and Peary were claiming to have reached the top of the world. He never achieved his dream of his own polar expedition. In 1916 he returned to New York. He claimed to have a story to tell about both Cook's and Peary's efforts. He offered to sell his story for a million dollars. There were no takers.

---

[23] "Eskimo Boy, First to Take College Course, Will Seek North Pole," *The Evening Telegram* (New York, January 22, 1909).

Robert Peary, the Inughuit, and the Iron Mountain

Polar explorer Robert Peary had studied the narratives of earlier explorers to the High Arctic before he first went among the Inughuit—the Polar Inuit of northwestern Greenland—for his over-wintering in 1891. He wasn't terribly impressed with what he read. Many other explorers had disparaged Inuit travel methods and had chosen to cart along all the food that they thought they might need. Peary thought it would make far more sense to use the dogs of the Inuit as his means of power, and the Inuit themselves to hunt for fresh meat for themselves, his party, and the dogs. So his first winter was, in essence, an experiment to see if his ideas about living, to a certain extent, off the land and the efforts of Inuit hunters were practical. He found that they were.

Still, some of his actions amused the Inuit. When he came back in 1893, this time to over-winter for two years, he brought donkeys on the ship to haul the expedition supplies from the beach to the site he had chosen to build his headquarters. He also brought his wife. He was the only explorer who had ever brought a woman so far north. Moreover, she was pregnant. Their first child, Marie Ahnighito, was born farther north than any white person had ever been born.

A Peary biographer gushed praise for his efforts:

"He learned to drive and care for dogs in native fashion. . . . He learned to dress like an Eskimo. . . . He learned the technique of building a snow-igloo. . . . He learned the value of laying in a supply of fresh meat during the proper hunting seasons. . . . He learned where game was most plentiful by listening to native teaching, and what methods of search were most successful. He discovered the psychology of the native, and so was able to organize the tribe almost with the efficacy he would have used with a large band of trained white helpers."

Perhaps Peary integrated himself with the Inuit a little too well, certainly more than his wife expected. Once Josephine and their child were back in the south, Peary carried on a relationship for many years with a young woman, Aleqasina. She was, of course, married to one of the hunters whom Peary commandeered at will and moved about like his own chattels every time he was in the district. His relationship with her began when she was only fifteen years old and resulted in two children, Saamik and Kaali.

In Those Days

(It was my privilege to know Kaali as a kind and helpful old man when I lived in Qaanaaq in the early 1980s.)

Although Peary thought the Inuit were a means to an end, he certainly did not look upon them as his equals. He wrote about them as "my faithful, trusty Eskimo allies, dusky children of the Pole," and "effective instruments for Arctic work." In one remarkable passage, he even wrote:

"I have often been asked: 'Of what use are Eskimos to the world?' They are too far removed to be of any value for commercial enterprises; and, furthermore, they lack ambition. They have no literature; nor, properly speaking, any art. They value life only as does a fox, or a bear, purely by instinct. But let us not forget that these people, trustworthy and hardy, will yet prove their value to mankind. With their help, the world shall discover the Pole."

The Inuit called him Piuli (the best they could do at pronouncing his name) or Piulirriaq—the great Peary. Uutaaq, who accompanied him on his final attempt on the North Pole, called him "a great leader" and was his friend. But a respected hunter, Imiina, reminiscing about him in 1967, called him "the great tormentor" and said, "People were afraid of him . . . really afraid. . . . He was a great leader. You always had the feeling that if you didn't do what he wanted, he would condemn you to death." In describing Peary having the contents of a barrel of biscuits thrown out on the beach for the Inuit to scramble for, Imiina commented, "My heart still turns cold to think of it. That scene tells very well how he considered this people—my people—who were, for all of that, devoted to him."

And so the relationship between Robert Peary and the Inughuit (some of whom are descended from the great man) was, and is, complex: one of respect, admiration, and fear. Peary too was torn, between his wife Josephine and his mistress Aleqasina, and between admiration for the Inughuit and the culture-bound beliefs of his time that said they must somehow be inferior to him because they were not white.

* * *

Perhaps no aspect of Peary's Northern explorations is so illustrative of his attitude to Inughuit and their property as his appropriation of their local source of iron.

John Ross was the first white explorer to encounter the Inughuit in their isolated corner of the High Arctic, in 1818. He observed with surprise that they used metal tools. They alone, of all Inuit, had discovered a local source of meteoric iron: three meteorites that were located about thirty-five miles to the east of Cape York, a place that would in later years become a meeting point for explorers or whalers, and Inughuit anxious to trade.

Ross and his fellow officers were interested in the knives that their first Inuit visitors had carried, a few of which they acquired in trade. Although the Inuit had never bartered with, or even met, white men before, their knives contained pieces of iron. Alexander Fisher, assistant surgeon, described them as being "made of small pieces, or plates of iron, which were set close together in a groove made in a piece of narwhal's horn; the end piece was riveted, but the others were kept in their places merely by being tightly driven into the groove."

A few days later, a group of Inuit again visited the ship, which was becalmed in Prince Regent's Bay. Using the West Greenlander Sakeouse as interpreter, Ross questioned one man, Meigack, about the iron. The Inuit's only purpose in travelling so far from their own country farther to the north, he told the interpreter, was to procure some of this iron, "which they break off with great difficulty by the means of stones, and then beat out into the small plates of which the knives are made." Alexander Fisher gave a detailed account; he reported that "they said that there were two . . . masses of it, the largest of which they described as being about the size of the skylight over Captain Ross's cabin, which is about four feet across. The other mass was reported by them to be considerably smaller." It came, Meigack said, from a place called Sowallick, a day's sled journey distant, at least twenty-five miles away. Despite the orthography, the word is easily recognizable as "Savilik"—the place with iron.

Ross regretted that time and ice conditions prevented him from sending a party to survey the area. His orders were to search for a Northwest Passage, not meteoric iron on the shores of Greenland. He would have to be content with the few knives he had bought and the information he had collected.

He returned to England that fall, and thus was born the myth of an "Iron Mountain" in northern Greenland.

* * *

After Ross's time, other expeditions set out in search of the iron mountain. Usually it was a secondary objective of a whaling or exploring expedition. In 1883 the Swedish-Finnish geologist and explorer Baron Adolf Erik Nordenskiöld's expedition tried to reach Cape York to discover and bring back the meteorites, but ice prevented them from reaching the site.

Robert Peary first heard about the meteorites in 1892 from Qisuk, one of his regular hunters and dog drivers. But just as the Inuit had been reluctant to tell John Ross where the meteorites were located, so too they were hesitant to share their secret with Peary. In both cases, they expected the white men to try to deprive them of their treasure. It was true that in the years since Ross's expedition, the waters of north Greenland had come to be frequented by whalers—the *upernaallit,* those who come in spring, as they called them—and that these men from far-off Scotland traded metal implements to the Inuit in return for furs and ivory. But what if they ceased coming? What if the Inuit needed to rely again on their hidden source of iron? And so they guarded their secret.

The Inuit had legends about these meteorites. Collectively they were called the *Saviksuit*—the great irons. Peary recounted what he had heard about them from the Inuit:

They were originally an Innuit [*sic*] woman and her dog and tent hurled from the sky by Tornarsuk (the Evil Spirit). They say that at first the "woman" was in shape like a woman seated and sewing, but that the constant chipping of fragments through successive ages has gradually removed the upper portion of her body and reduced her size one-half or one-third.

Years ago her head became detached and a party of Eskimos from Peterahwik [Pitoraarfik] or Etah [Iita] (settlements north of Whale Sound) attempted to carry it away, actuated probably by the desire to have a supply of the precious metal more convenient, and save themselves the long and arduous journey to Cape York and into Melville Bay, when they needed to replenish their stock of iron. The head was lashed upon a sledge and the party started for their home, but when well out from the shore the sea ice suddenly broke up with a loud noise, and the head disappeared beneath the water, dragging down with it the sledge and dogs. The Eskimos narrowly escaped with their lives, and since that time no attempt has been made to carry away any but the smallest fragments of the heavenly woman.[24]

Finally, in May of 1894, Peary badgered one man, Aleqatsiaq, to take him to the meteorites. When they reached the site, they dug away the snow to reveal a large brown mass. Aleqatsiaq proclaimed it to be the headless woman.

Peary spent the following day measuring, sketching, and photographing the treasure. Then, in an act of supreme arrogance, he carved a rough "P" on the metallic surface. This was, he said, "an indisputable proof of my having found the meteorite." Apparently, the fact that Inuit had known about it all along counted for nothing.

Aleqatsiaq also showed Peary the site of the largest of the meteorites, called "the tent," on Bushnan Island, but deep snow prevented him from actually setting eyes on it.

Peary wondered which had arrived first on the peninsula at Cape York: the Inuit or the meteorite. He concluded that it must have been the Inuit, because their legends referred to the meteorites being "hurled from the sky." Some generations before, he thought, Inuit had seen a shower of fiery balls streak across the night sky. The spirits were angry. It was a fortuitous coincidence that Inuit subsequently chanced upon the site where some of these objects had struck the earth.

---

[24] Robert E. Peary, *Northward over the "Great Ice,"* Vol. II (New York: Frederick A. Stokes Company, 1898), 559, 561.

Back at his headquarters at Anniversary Lodge, Peary began planning how to make the meteorites, all of them, his own. He would take them back to America and use them to raise cash to finance future expeditions.

* * *

He told his wife, who had wintered in Greenland with him, "This means that if the ship comes I can get one or two of the meteorites aboard her. By their sale or exhibition your brother . . . can raise enough to send a ship next year."

His ship, the *Falcon*, did come, but ice prevented her from reaching the site. Peary remained in the Arctic for a second winter, having sent his wife and daughter home on the ship. The next summer, after the arrival of a steamer, the *Kite*, Peary reached Cape York in August. With the help of a crew of Inuit, he and his men loaded the meteorites known as the "woman" and the "dog," their weights estimated respectively at three tons and one thousand pounds, and hauled them away to America.

Back in Brooklyn, Peary again took up his job with the United States Navy. But he was also busy planning to return to Greenland to retrieve the largest meteorite, the "tent." Bad weather ensured that the next summer's voyage, on a ship called *Hope*, was only a partial success. The "tent" was excavated with great difficulty and moved to the shore before the pack ice of Melville Bay, the ice that had spelled doom to so many previous ships in these treacherous waters, drove in on the land. The *Hope* retreated hastily, leaving the exposed "tent" to await another season.

In 1897 Peary returned to northern Greenland, again on the *Hope*. This time ice conditions were favourable, and the little vessel reached Cape York on August 12. The previous year he had told some of his most trusted Inuit hunters and guides, among them Qisuk and Nuktaq, to meet him at the cape the following summer, and they had not failed him. All the able-bodied men waiting at Cape York boarded the ship and set off for Bushnan Island. The challenge there was to load the largest meteorite—the only one remaining—aboard the tiny ship. The task was monumental, as was the object itself. Peary estimated that the "tent" weighed between ninety and one hundred tons. He exaggerated, of course, but still, it weighed 37.5 tons.

The captain berthed the *Hope* alongside a natural rock pier on Meteorite Island, as Peary called Bushnan Island. Peary described his plans for loading his treasure:

"I proposed to construct a very strong bridge, reaching from the shore across the ship; lay the heaviest steel rails upon this, and then, after depositing the meteorite upon a massive timber car resting upon these rails, slide the huge mass across the bridge until it rested directly over the main hatch; remove the bridge; then lower the meteorite with my hydraulic jacks through the hatchway to the ship's hold."

And that, in a nutshell, is what he did, although the entire operation took six days. Not one to miss a photo op, Peary had the meteorite draped in the Stars and Stripes. As it started its inch-by-inch ride across the improvised bridge toward the ship, Peary's daughter, who, with her mother, was along for the summer cruise, smashed a bottle of wine against it and named it Ahnighito. This was the little girl, Marie Peary's, middle name, rendered in Peary's clumsy spelling. The Pearys made much of the fact that the name had been given to their daughter by the Inuit at the time of her birth in northern Greenland—it should properly be spelled

Arnakittoq in Greenlandic—and that it meant "the snow baby." In fact it means "small woman" or "small female." The name stuck, and the largest meteorite ever recovered became known not as the tent, but as Ahnighito.

As the meteorite neared the edge of the vessel, the Inuit left the ship, superstitious perhaps, or simply fearing that the weight of the stone might crush the ship were any accident to happen. But the meteorite was safely loaded.

With the cargo securely aboard, the *Hope* steamed for Cape York, where most of the Inuit were put ashore and paid for their work. "I sent my faithful Eskimos ashore," Peary wrote, "accompanied by several barrels of biscuit, and loaded with guns, knives, ammunition, and numerous other articles which I had brought to reward them for their faithful service."

Six Inuit, though, didn't disembark. They travelled to New York with Peary, with tragic results. Their fate is documented in my book, *Minik: The New York Eskimo*, originally published as *Give Me My Father's Body: The Life of Minik, the New York Eskimo*. As for the meteorites, it would take some time for Peary to recoup the money invested in the multi-year project that deprived the Inuit of their source of iron. But ultimately, he found a way.

He decided that the meteorites would have a home in the American Museum of Natural History, and that he would be paid handsomely for them. He set the stage for the museum's acquisition of the treasures by taking along with him on two of his expeditions an artist, Albert Operti, who would plan a museum setting that would have all the Cape York meteorites displayed with scenes from the lives of the Inuit.

At the conclusion of each expedition that recovered meteorites, the treasures arrived at the museum amid much publicity. Of

143

course, the public saw them as a generous gift from a man dedicated to the cause of Arctic science. What they did not know was that the meteorites were merely on long-term loan, pending a sale.

It took a number of years for the grasping explorer to collect his payment. But finally, while he was away in Greenland on his last expedition, his wife sold the meteorites to the museum for $50,000. This was a fabulous sum a century ago. But there was no publicity accompanying this major museum acquisition, for the public had thought all along that the museum already owned the exhibits that attracted so many visitors. The Pearys had quietly gotten paid.

Minik, the New York Eskimo

A Victim of Peary's Neglect

Perhaps nothing is more illustrative of the cavalier attitude of many explorers to the Indigenous people who made their efforts a success than the callous actions of Robert Peary to the six Inughuit he took to New York in 1897, actions that had long-term consequences in the life of a young Inuit boy.

Minik's story is the true story of a young Greenlander, about seven years of age, who was taken to New York with his father and four other Inuit from the farthest northern reaches of Greenland by Robert Peary. Peary's purpose? To turn them over to the American Museum of Natural History for exhibition. Predictably, four of them died within a few months, including Minik's father. A young male survivor was sent back north the following year, but Minik was kept in the United States for the next twelve years. Peary denied any responsibility in the matter.

Minik lived with the family of William Wallace, the museum's building superintendent, and received an education. He learned to swim and loved to ride horseback. Most of all, he loved baseball, and he even took up golf as a teenager. Despite his physical activities, he was often ill, and in and out of hospital.

In 1901 things changed. William Wallace was fired by the museum—he had been caught taking bribes from building contractors. The family fell on hard times. Morris Jesup, the wealthy president of the museum, who had promised to help Wallace with funds for Minik's education, refused any more help for the boy. Then in 1904 Wallace's wife, Minik's beloved foster mother, died. Strangely, Wallace sent his own son away to live with relatives, but kept Minik living with him. But it was now a pauper's existence.

In 1906 things got worse, not financially, but emotionally. Minik learned that his father's body had not been buried after he died in 1898. Instead it had been defleshed, and the skeleton put on display in the American Museum of Natural History.

But how could this be? wondered Minik. He was there when his father was buried. How was it possible that his father's skeleton could be in a glass case in the museum?

The truth was shocking. The museum had staged a sham funeral for the sole purpose of convincing Minik that his father was being buried. The people that Minik had trusted the most were all in on the deception, including the famous anthropologist Franz Boas, and Minik's beloved foster father, William Wallace.

In fact, Wallace later provided a description of the events of that tragic night. He said:

That night some of us gathered on the museum grounds by order of the scientific staff, and got an old log about the length of a human corpse. This was wrapped in cloth, a mask attached to one end of it and all was in readiness.

Dusk was the time chosen for the mock burial, as there was some fear of attracting too much attention from the street. . . . Then, too, the boy would be less apt to discover the ruse. The funeral party knew the act must be accomplished quickly and quietly, so about the time the lights began to flare up Minik was taken out on the grounds, where the imitation body was placed on the ground and a mound of stones piled on top of it after the Eskimo fashion.

While Minik stood sobbing by, the museum men lingered around watching the proceedings. The thing worked well. The boy never suspected.[25]

But eventually Minik learned the truth, and it devastated him. He launched a campaign to have his father's skeleton released from the museum. "Give Me My Father's Body" was the title of a full-page newspaper article about Minik's desire to give his father's remains a decent burial. But he was unsuccessful. In 1909, disillusioned by his life in America, he returned to northern Greenland.

Back home, Minik was like a fish out of water. He couldn't speak Inuktun, nor did he know how to hunt. But under the expert tutelage of relatives—among them an ancient shaman, Soqqaq, and the renowned Uutaaq, the leader of the group of Inuit who had accompanied Peary to his farthest north—Minik learned fast

---

[25] "Why Mene, Young Eskimo Boy, Ran Away from his Home," *New York Evening Mail* (April 21, 1909): 1, column 4.

and well. When another American expedition arrived three years later, Minik was in demand as an interpreter and guide.

When I was researching Minik's life, I talked with a number of elders in Qaanaaq and Siorapaluk who had known him when they were young. One thing they all marvelled at was how quickly he had relearned his language and hunting skills.

But, just as he had longed for Greenland when he was in America, so now he yearned for New York when he was back in Greenland. He returned south in 1916. Two years later he died in the Spanish flu epidemic that swept the world. He was about twenty-eight years old. He is buried in New Hampshire, just south of the Canadian border.

* * *

For almost a century, the bones of Minik's father, Qisuk, and those of the other Inuit taken to New York, Nuktaq, Atangana, and Aviaq, remained in a box on a shelf in the American Museum of Natural History under accession number 99/3610.

In 1986, with the publication of my book on Minik's life, the museum was embarrassed. It had succeeded in covering up the story of Minik and its treatment of the remains of Qisuk and his fellow Inuit for the better part of a century. But coverups would no longer work. After publication, periodic newspaper articles about Minik and the bones of his father reminded the public and the museum about the story. In particular, a front-page article in 1992 in the *Globe and Mail* and another in the *Washington Post* brought knowledge of the injustice to the public eye again.

This time the interest in having the bones removed from the museum remained high. Since 1986, things had changed in the conservative world of American museums. American Indians had made progress in forcing museums to deal appropriately with the remains of their ancestors.

In 1990 the Native American Grave and Burial Protection Act was passed. Under that legislation, American museums are required to return skeletal remains to native groups that request them and have a valid claim on them. Qisuk and the other Inughuit, however, were not covered by this legislation. They were Greenlanders, not Americans, and the American Museum of Natural History was under no obligation to send their bones to Greenland or anywhere else for burial.

But the museum authorities had had enough.

On July 28, 1993, the bones of the four Polar Inuit were loaded aboard an American military transport aircraft at Maguire Air Force Base in New Jersey and transported to Thule Air Base in northern Greenland. The journey that had taken over a month in 1897 was accomplished in a few short hours. At Thule, the cargo was transferred to a Greenlandair helicopter for the trip to Qaanaaq, less than an hour away.

Officialdom almost had one last surprise for the souls of the four returning Inuit. The Lutheran Church had decided that, because the Inuit were pagans and unbaptized, they could not be buried in a Christian ceremony. That decision, however, was quickly reconsidered, and the bodies were received at the small church in Qaanaaq.

On August 1 the bodies, each in its own small casket, were placed in a common grave in hallowed ground on a hillside with a splendid view of the sea to the west. Rocks were piled on top of the grave in the traditional manner. In the presence of about one hundred local residents, a brief service was held at the graveside. Three people spoke: the priest, Hans Johan Lennert; the mayor of the community, August Eipe; and Edmund Carpenter, a self-serving, egotistical representative of the American Museum of Natural History.

Mayor August Eipe referred to "the long-sought final resting place of our ancestors Qisuk, Nuktaq, Atangana and Aviaq." He noted that they had "against their will, helped to write our history."

The vicar, Hans Johan Lennert, observing that "life was not kind to these people," went on to say that "through their life stories . . . we have gained great knowledge and understanding of many things."

His words presaged the peculiar remarks of Edmund Carpenter, who described the four dead Inuit as volunteers in a noble quest for knowledge:

> Museums of natural history were founded on the belief that all life belongs to a common order subject to common principles. There is the further belief that science can contribute to human betterment. To this end, scientists gather information from many lands.
>
> It was in this spirit that citizens from this area visited New York nearly a century ago. There they contributed details of their customs and beliefs to this grand pursuit of knowledge. They did not live to know the importance of their contribution, but we do, and it should not be forgotten.[26]

"Visited?" "Contributed?" These were not the sentiments that the mayor had just expressed on behalf of the community of Qaanaaq.

---

[26] Division of Anthropology Archives, American Museum of Natural History, "Burial Service, Qaanaaq, Greenland. 8/1/93. Edmund Carpenter and Adelaide de Menil" (press release).

Carpenter, a wealthy patron of the museum, was a pushy man, and accustomed to using his wife's considerable fortune to buy his way into situations that fed his enormous ego. Four years later he published an article in which he restated the contribution that Qisuk and his fellow deceased had made to science. Describing them as "ethnographic and linguistic informants"—again implying that they had travelled to New York voluntarily—he noted, "Their bodies were measured and cast. When four died, their skeletons were measured. An autopsy was performed on one. . . . These findings helped Boas challenge racism."

He elaborated: "Knowledge gained from these six Polar Eskimos challenged that belief."

For Carpenter, then, it was all right. The ends justified the means. Four Inuit died agonizing, unnecessary deaths, but science—perhaps all of mankind—benefited, and to him that justified the unwilling sacrifice they had made.

A plaque was provided for eventual erection at the gravesite. It began with the terse statement, "NUNAMINGNUT UTEQIHUT." It translates simply as "They have come home." This statement is followed by the names of the four Inuit with details of their births and deaths and the statement "1897 NEW YORK-IMUT, 1993 QAANAAMUT."

On August 4, 1997, one hundred years after Qisuk, Nuktaq, Atangana, and Aviaq left the Thule district for New York aboard the *Hope*, and four years after the return of their remains to Greenland and their burial in the graveyard at Qaanaaq, the memorial plaque was finally placed over their common grave. Queen Margrethe of Denmark and her husband, Prince Henrik, attended its unveiling in a touching ceremony presided over

In Those Days

by the mayor, Lars Jeremiassen, who spoke of the community's wish to honour their forefathers who loved their living and grieved their dead.

FIGURE 1: Portrait of Martin Frobisher.
SOURCE: THE BODLEIAN LIBRARY, UNIVERSITY OF OXFORD,
L.P. 50.

Homme sauuage amene des païs Septentrionaux par M. Furbisher L'an 1576

FIGURE 2: A watercolour of Frobisher's Inuk captive by Lucas de Heere (1534-1584), who was from Ghent, Belgium, but worked in London. The exact date of the painting is unknown. It is also not known if he painted the man from life, or from the work (now lost) of another Flemish painter, Cornelis Ketel, who is known to have painted the man.

SOURCE: RIJKSUNIVERSITEIT GENT (GHENT UNIVERSITY LIBRARY BHSL.HS.2466).

FIGURE 3: Inuit and Frobisher's men fought a battle, at which several Inuit were killed, at Bloody Point in Frobisher Bay in 1577. The picture is by or after John White.
SOURCE: BRITISH MUSEUM 00026164001.

FIGURE 4: In 1577 Frobisher captured a man, woman, and child, and took them to England where all three died. The man's name has been recorded as "Calichoe" or "Callichogh." This contemporary picture of him is by John White.
SOURCE: BRITISH MUSEUM 00025919001.

FIGURE 5: The woman abducted in Frobisher Bay and taken to England in 1577 was named "Egnoge" or "Ignorth," probably an attempt to write "Arnaq" (woman). The child was called "Nutioc," which was probably "Nutaraq" (child). The drawing is by John White.
SOURCE: BRITISH MUSEUM 00099113001.

FIGURE 6: In 1611 the crew of Henry Hudson's ship, *Discovery*, mutinied; they cast Hudson, his son, and seven other men adrift in a small boat in Hudson Bay.
SOURCE: THE LAST VOYAGE OF HENRY HUDSON, EXHIBITED 1881, THE HON. JOHN COLLIER (1850-1934) TATE, LONDON 2015. ITEM NO. NO1616.

FIGURE 7: A sketch by Uqijjuaqsi Nanuq, showing herself performing devotions at an ancient monument erected by Qallunaat on the shores of Frobisher Bay. The lines around the top of the monument are strings to which the Inuit hung offerings to secure good luck in hunting.

SOURCE: CHARLES FRANCIS HALL. *LIFE WITH THE ESQUIMAUX*, VOLUME II. LONDON: SAMPSON, LOW, SON, AND MARSTON, 1864, PAGE 285.

FIGURE 8: Samuel Hearne led a Hudson's Bay Company expedition to the Coppermine River in 1771. It resulted in the slaughter of a group of Inuit.

SOURCE: GLENBOW ARCHIVES, NA-3548-1.

MATONABBEE TRAVELLING NORTH/MATONABBEE S'AVENTURE AU NORD

FIGURE 9: In 1989, Canada issued a postage stamp honouring Matonabbee, the leader of the party of Chipewyans who perpetrated the massacre of Inuit at Bloody Fall, near the mouth of the Coppermine River.

SOURCE: CANADA POST CORPORATION 1989. REPRODUCED WITH PERMISSION.

FIGURE 10: A group of Inuit at Iglulik. This illustration is from William Edward Parry's narrative, published in 1824. It is from a drawing by George Lyon, engraved by Edward Finden.

SOURCE: WILLIAM EDWARD PARRY: *JOURNAL OF A SECOND VOYAGE FOR THE DISCOVERY OF A NORTH-WEST PASSAGE*. LONDON: JOHN MURRAY, 1824, FACING PAGE 418.

FIGURE 11: Inuit children dancing. From a drawing by George Lyon. Iglulik 1823.

SOURCE: WILLIAM EDWARD PARRY: *JOURNAL OF A SECOND VOYAGE FOR THE DISCOVERY OF A NORTH-WEST PASSAGE*. LONDON: JOHN MURRAY, 1824, FACING PAGE 530.

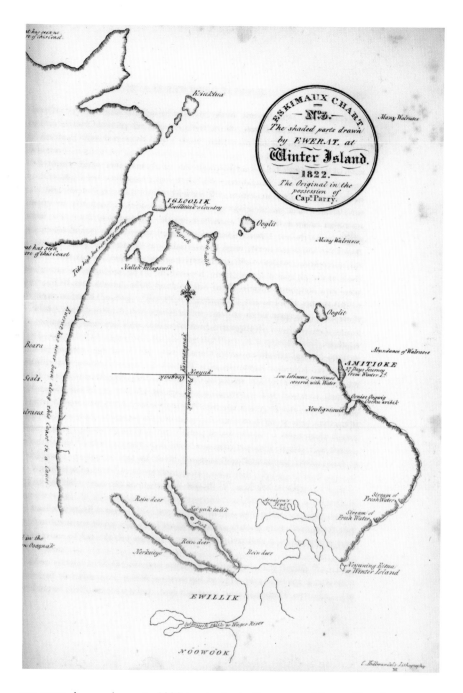

FIGURE 12: A map drawn in 1822 by the Inuk, Ewerat, and Parry. The shaded parts of the coastline were drawn by Ewerat, the rest and the notes by Parry. "Ewerat" may be Parry's attempt to write the name "Ujaraq." Early explorers were impressed by the map-making abilities of Inuit.

SOURCE: WILLIAM EDWARD PARRY: *JOURNAL OF A SECOND VOYAGE FOR THE DISCOVERY OF A NORTH-WEST PASSAGE.* LONDON: JOHN MURRAY, 1824, FACING PAGE 252.

FIGURE 13: A group of Inuit encountered by Parry and Lyon in 1822, south of the Iglulik area.

SOURCE: WILLIAM EDWARD PARRY: *JOURNAL OF A SECOND VOYAGE FOR THE DISCOVERY OF A NORTH-WEST PASSAGE*. LONDON: JOHN MURRAY, 1824, FACING PAGE 163.

FIGURE 14: The explorer George Back had medals made as gifts for the Inuit on his 1836-1837 expedition to discover the Northwest Passage. They bore the inscription "H.M.S. TERROR 1836 CAPTN BACK 1836," and had a hole so they could be worn as a necklace. William Edward Parry had similar medals made on his winterings in Foxe Basin in 1821-1823, none of which are known to have survived.

SOURCE: NATIONAL MARITIME MUSEUM (ENGLAND), OBJECT ID MEC2748. PHOTO COURTESY OF DR. RUSSELL POTTER.

FIGURE 15: Tatannuaq was an Inuk from the Kivalliq coast who learned to speak English at the Hudson Bay Company's Churchill post. He served John Franklin on both his overland expeditions in northwestern Canada in the 1820s. Franklin always referred to him as Augustus

SOURCE: KENN HARPER COLLECTION.

FIGURE 16: Hiutiruq, also known as Junius, from the Hudson Bay coast
north of Churchill, accompanied Tatannuaq on John Franklin's first
overland expedition in 1921.

SOURCE: KENN HARPER COLLECTION.

FIGURE 17: A portrait of Sir John Ross, from a picture by B. R. Faulkner. Ross met the isolated Nattilingmiut on a voyage in search of a Northwest Passage, with his nephew James Clark Ross on the *Victory*, 1829-1833

SOURCE: KENN HARPER COLLECTION.

FIGURE 18: Two Inuit, Ikmalick and Apelagliu, visited John Ross in his cabin on the *Victory*. Ikmalick was a skilled cartographer and is shown explaining a map to the explorers.

SOURCE: SIR JOHN ROSS. *NARRATIVE OF A SECOND VOYAGE IN SEARCH OF A NORTH-WEST PASSAGE...* LONDON: A. W. WEBSTER, 1835, FACING PAGE 260.

FIGURE 19: Awtigin was one of the Inuit encountered by Sir John Ross on the Boothia Peninsula. He is shown here, in a rendering by Ross, with his two wives Udlia and Palurak

SOURCE: SIR JOHN ROSS. *APPENDIX TO THE NARRATIVE OF A SECOND VOYAGE IN SEARCH OF A NORTH-WEST PASSAGE...* LONDON: A. W. WEBSTER, 1835, FACING PAGE 49.

FIGURE 20: Sir John Ross made this sketch of Tulluahiu and his wife Tirikshiu and daughter Shulanina. Tulluahiu is wearing the wooden leg carved for him by the carpenter of the *Victory*.
SOURCE: SIR JOHN ROSS. *NARRATIVE OF A SECOND VOYAGE IN SEARCH OF A NORTH-WEST PASSAGE...* LONDON: A. W. WEBSTER, 1835, FACING PAGE 272.

FIGURE 21: Qaqortingneq (right), who led Knud Rasmussen in 1923 to a site on the Adelaide Peninsula where they found skeletal remains of members of the lost Franklin expedition. He is seen here with Rasmussen's travelling companion, Qaavigarsuaq, from northern Greenland.
SOURCE: KNUD RASMUSSEN. *REPORT OF THE FIFTH THULE EXPEDITION (1921-1924): THE NETSILIK ESKIMOS. SOCIAL LIFE AND SPIRITUAL CULTURE.* VOL. VII, NO. 1, COPENHAGEN: GYLDENDALSKE BOGHANDEL, 1931, FACING PAGE 409.

FIGURE 22: Iggiaraarjuk, a Nattilik man who told Rasmussen of his father's meeting with three men of the Franklin expedition on King William Island.

SOURCE: KNUD RASMUSSEN. *REPORT OF THE FIFTH THULE EXPEDITION (1921-1924): THE NETSILIK ESKIMOS. SOCIAL LIFE AND SPIRITUAL CULTURE.* VOL. VII, NO. 1, COPENHAGEN: GYLDENDALSKE BOGHANDEL, 1931, FACING PAGE 85.

FIGURE 23: Knud Rasmussen travelled through the central Arctic on the Fifth Thule Expedition (1921-1924), documenting the folklore and spiritual practices of Canadian Inuit. From Nattilingmiut, he learned of the fate of the Franklin expedition

SOURCE: KENN HARPER COLLECTION.

FIGURE 24: John Rae, pictured here, was an Orkney man who worked for the Hudson's Bay Company. He travelled with Inuit, including Albert One-Eye, and William Ouligbuck Senior and Junior.

SOURCE: KENN HARPER COLLECTION.

FIGURE 25: William Ouligbuck Junior was an interpreter and guide from the Kivalliq region who was indispensable to the explorer John Rae in discovering the fate of some of the men of the Franklin expedition.
SOURCE: PHOTOGRAPH BY GEORGE SIMPSON MCTAVISH, FROM GEORGE SIMPSON MCTAVISH'S *BEHIND THE PALISADES*, PRIVATELY PUBLISHED, 1963.

FIGURE 26: Tookoolito (Hannah) and her husband Ipiirvik (Ebierbing, Joe), posed with explorer Charles Francis Hall.
SOURCE: CHARLES FRANCIS HALL. *ARCTIC RESEARCHES AND LIFE AMONG THE ESQUIMAUX*. NEW YORK: HARPER & BROS., 1864, FRONTISPIECE.

FIGURE 27: Ipiirvik, known to explorers as Ebierbing or Esquimaux Joe, posed in a photographer's studio in New England between expeditions.

SOURCE: J. E. NOURSE. *NARRATIVE OF THE SECOND ARCTIC EXPEDITION MADE BY C. F. HALL.* WASHINGTON: GOVERNMENT PRINTING OFFICE, 1879, FACING PAGE 443.

JOE, HANNAH, AND CHILD.

FIGURE 28: Ipiirvik (known to whalers as Joe), Tookoolito (known as Hannah), and their child, Panik (known as Sylvia Grinnell) pose in a studio in the United States in the 1860s.

SOURCE: KENN HARPER COLLECTION.

FIGURE 29: Three headstones for Inuit are in the Starr Burying Ground in Groton, Connecticut. Tookoolito's monument, bearing her English name Hannah, stands in the background. Her daughter Panik (Sylvia Grinnell Ebierbing) is to the right foreground. Three Inuit names are on the marker to the left, but only "Tukilikitar" is buried there; the other two names are of Inuit who died aboard ship and are memorialized there.

SOURCE: KENN HARPER COLLECTION.

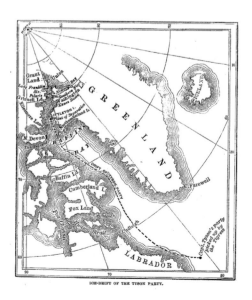

FIGURE 30: In October 1872 a party of Inuit and Qallunaat, nineteen people in total, drifted away from the ship, *Polaris*, on the ice in a storm. They drifted for over six months and 1,500 miles until they were rescued by a sealer north of Newfoundland. Because the two Inuit men were able to hunt to provide food, there was no loss of life.

SOURCE: KENN HARPER COLLECTION.

FIGURE 31: The group that drifted on the ice floe included two Inuit families. One was Ipiirvik and Tookoolito and their daughter, Panik. The other was a Greenlander, Hans Hendrik, and his wife and children. They are pictured here in a St. John's photographer's studio after their rescue.
SOURCE: KENN HARPER COLLECTION.

FIGURE 32: In 1897 Robert Peary took four Inuit to the United States. They were photographed the following year on the steps of a house in Lawyersville in New York State. From left to right are Nuktaq, Uisaakassak, Minik, and Minik's father Qisuk.
SOURCE: KENN HARPER COLLECTION.

FIGURE 33: Minik in America in 1898.
SOURCE: KENN HARPER COLLECTION.

FIGURE 34: In New York, Minik lived much like an American boy. He is pictured here with his bicycle.

SOURCE: KENN HARPER COLLECTION.

FIGURE 35: In 1993 the skeletal remains of four Inuit who had died in America were taken to Qaanaaq, Greenland for burial. They were Minik's father Qisuk, Nuktaq, Atangana, and Aviaq.

SOURCE: PHOTOGRAPH BY KENN HARPER.

FIGURE 36: Minik died in New Hampshire in 1918. He is buried there in a quiet cemetery outside the village of Pittsburg.

SOURCE: PHOTOGRAPH BY KENN HARPER.

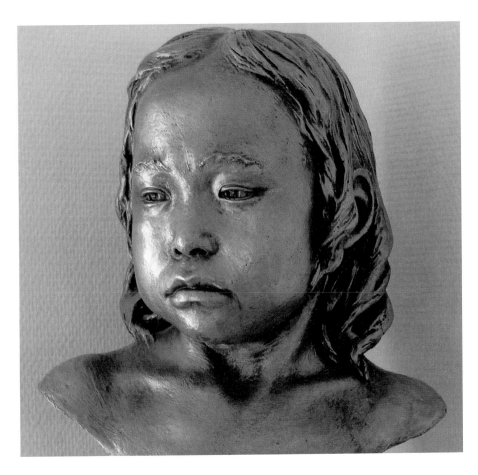

FIGURE 37: A bust of Minik, a replica of one in the American Museum of Natural History, occupies a place of prominence in the municipal office in Qaanaaq, Greenland.

SOURCE: PHOTOGRAPH BY KENN HARPER.

FIGURE 38: Uutaaq, sometimes written as Odak or Otak, was the leader of the four Inughuit who accompanied Robert Peary and Matthew Henson on an expedition that Peary claimed reached the North Pole.

SOURCE: PHOTO BY ERIK HOLTVED, ARKTISK INSTITUT (DENMARK), #125309.

FIGURE 39: Uutaaq in old age. Uutaaq accompanied Robert Peary to his farthest north in 1909.

SOURCE: KENN HARPER COLLECTION.

FIGURE 40: Robert Peary, posed here in his naval uniform, claimed to have reached the North Pole in 1909, travelling with four Inughuit and a Black servant.
SOURCE: KENN HARPER COLLECTION.

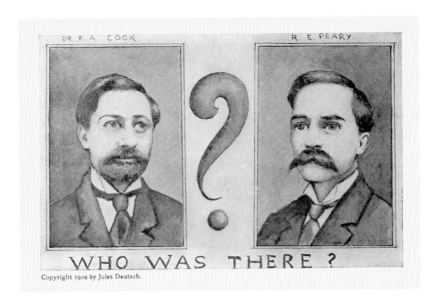

FIGURE 41: Both Peary and Cook claimed to have reached the North Pole, each with Inuit assistance. They fought their battle in the press. Companies brought out postcards supporting the claims of one or the other, and sometimes both. This is a postcard by the Jules Deutsch company.
SOURCE: KENN HARPER COLLECTION.

FIGURE 42: Qitdlugtoq, sometimes written as Kudlooktoo, who shot Peary's assistant, Ross Marvin, because of his irrational behaviour toward his Inuit travelling companions.
SOURCE: COURTESY STEPHEN LORING, ARCTIC STUDIES CENTER, SMITHSONIAN INSTITUTION.

FIGURE 43: Dr. Frederick Cook claimed to have reached the geographic North Pole in 1908, one year before Robert Peary claimed the same accomplishment. Cook travelled with two young Inuit men, Ittukusuk and Aapilak.
SOURCE: KENN HARPER COLLECTION.

FIGURE 44: Matthew Henson, seen here in Inuit costume, was Robert Peary's Black assistant for all the years Peary worked in Greenland. Henson had an Inuit wife and one son. He has numerous descendants in Greenland today.
SOURCE: KENN HARPER COLECTION.

FIGURE 45: Matthew Henson, Peary's assistant, in the United States after his and Peary's final expedition to Greenland

SOURCE: MATTHEW HENSON: *A NEGRO EXPLORER AT THE NORTH POLE*. NEW YORK: FREDERICK A. STOKES, 1912, FRONTISPIECE.

FIGURE 46: Donald Baxter MacMillan's first trip to the Arctic was with Peary in 1908-1909. He subsequently returned in 1913 on a four-year quest for the non-existent Crocker Land.

SOURCE: KENN HARPER COLLECTION.

FIGURE 47: Captain Joseph-Elzéar Bernier commanded three voyages to the High Arctic between 1906 and 1911. On each one, he impressed upon Inuit the fact that they were citizens of Canada, with rights and responsibilities.

FIGURE 48: Bernier continued his voyages to the High Arctic into old age. Here he is seen with returning prisoner Nuqallaq at Quebec City in 1925. Nuqallaq had served two years of a ten-year sentence for manslaughter.
SOURCE: LIBRARY AND ARCHIVES CANADA/DEPARTMENT OF INDIAN AFFAIRS AND NORTHERN DEVELOPMENT FONDS/C068629.

FIGURE 49: Makpii was an Inupiat Alaskan girl who went with her parents on the Canadian Arctic Expedition's ship *Karluk* in 1911 when she was only two years old. She survived the sinking of the ship, an escape over the ice to Wrangel Island off the coast of Siberia, and a winter there.
SOURCE: SIEFFERT FAMILY PHOTOGRAPHS COLLECTION, ALASKA AND POLAR REGIONS COLLECTIONS, ELMER E. RASMUSON LIBRARY, UNIVERSITY OF ALASKA, FAIRBANKS.

IDENTIFICATION NUMBER 1985-122-144.

FIGURE 50: Bob Bartlett was a Newfoundland-born captain who worked for explorers Peary and Stefansson. In 1911, when Stefansson's ship, *Karluk*, sank, Bartlett and his Alaskan Inupiat shipmates organized an escape over the ice to Wrangel Island. From there he and one Inupiat man travelled by dogsled to Nome to organize the party's rescue.

SOURCE: KENN HARPER COLLECTION.

FIGURE 51: Ada Blackjack, an Alaskan Inupiat woman, was the sole survivor of a disastrous two-year expedition, organized by Vilhjalmur Stefasson, to Wrangel Island, north of Siberia (1921-1923).

SOURCE: BOB BARTLETT. *THE LOG OF BOB BARTLETT,* NEW YORK: G. P. PUTNAM'S SONS, 1928, FACING PAGE 6.

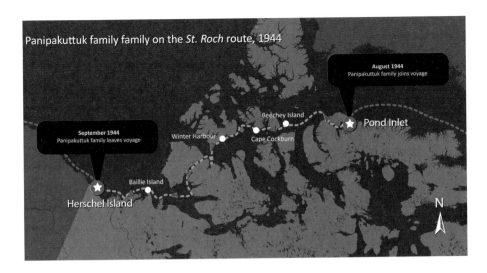

Panipakuttuk family family on the *St. Roch* route, 1944

August 1944
Panipakuttuk family joins voyage

Beechey Island

Pond Inlet

September 1944
Panipakuttuk family leaves voyage

Winter Harbour

Cape Cockburn

Baillie Island

Herschel Island

N

FIGURE 52: This map shows the travels of the Panipakuttuk family on the RCMP vessel *St. Roch* through the Northwest Passage from east to west in 1944.
SOURCE: PRINCE OF WALES NORTHERN HERITAGE CENTRE/ GOVERNMENT OF THE NORTHWEST TERRITORIES.

FIGURE 53: The Panipakuttuk family from Pond Inlet accompanied the *St. Roch* through the Northwest Passage in 1944. Letia Panipakuttuk, a seamstress, is seated in the centre with baby Elijah in her amauti. Her mother-in-law Panikpak is on the right.
SOURCE: ITEM NUMBER: HISG-40-01. VANCOUVER MARITIME MUSEUM.

FIGURE 54: Henry Larsen was a Norwegian-born RCMP officer who captained the *St. Roch* through the Northwest Passage on the voyage on which the Panipakuttuk family participated.

SOURCE: ITEM NUMBER: LM2016.999.003. VANCOUVER MARITIME MUSEUM

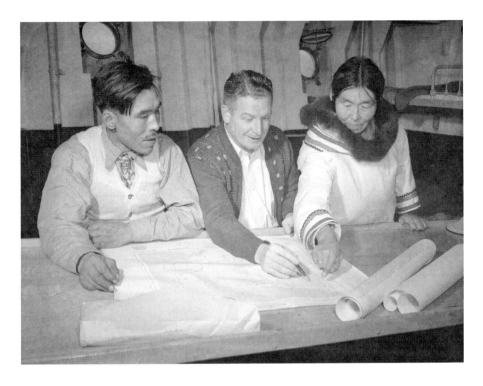

FIGURE 55: Joe Panipakutuk and his mother Panikpak show government administrator Alex Strevenson the location of a shipwreck, while en route to Craig Harbour in 1951.

FIGURE 56: In 1974, thirty years after the Panipakuttuk family went through the Northwest Passage, Joe Panipakuttuk's widow Letia received a Polar Medal on his behalf.

SOURCE: *INUKTITUT MAGAZINE,* WINTER 1975, COVER PHOTO.

FIGURE 57: A specimen of a Polar Medal.

SOURCE: COURTESY GLENN M. STEIN, FRGS, FRCGS.

I Will Find a Way or Fake One

Robert Peary Claims the North Pole

Robert Peary's single-minded eighteen-year quest for the North Pole dominated the lives of the Polar Inuit of northwestern Greenland, whom he recruited as assistants. One can't really call them "guides," since they had never been to the elusive destination before.

In 1891–92, he led an expedition that wintered in and explored northern Greenland. From 1893 to 1895, another expedition accomplished little but did succeed in taking two meteorites to New York. A summer voyage in 1896 accomplished nothing, but a voyage the following summer brought the largest of the meteorites to the American Museum of Natural History. In the longest expedition, Peary passed four consecutive winters in the far North, between 1898 and 1902, and made a serious but unsuccessful attempt on the North Pole. An over-wintering expedition in 1905–06 was similarly unsuccessful.

Finally, in 1908 Peary left the United States on his final expedition. After wintering on the north coast of Ellesmere Island, he and a number of support parties left in late winter for the Pole. In April of 1909, Peary's quest of almost two decades came to an end. He claimed that he reached the North Pole, the object of his driving ambition, on April 6.

He had wintered his ship, the *Roosevelt*, at Cape Sheridan, at the northern end of Ellesmere Island. In mid-February he put his plan, the "Peary System," into place. Support parties of Inuit, his own hand-picked Americans, and one Newfoundlander would go ahead according to a schedule devised by Peary. They would take provisions, mark a trail, and build snowhouse shelters for the final party, which would consist of Peary, Matthew Henson, and four Inuit.

Peary's party left the relative comfort of the ship on February 22. They skirted the northern coast of Ellesmere for a week, heading north, then west. On March 1 he finally left the coast at Cape Columbia and proceeded north. But at his fourth camp, he was halted by a stretch of open water, the famous "big lead." He was not able to make it across for another week.

The supporting parties that had preceded him turned back one by one. Dr. Goodsell's was the first, on March 14. The following day, Donald MacMillan and his party turned back. Five days later it was George Borup's turn to reverse direction and begin the journey back to the ship. On March 26, the ill-fated Ross Marvin, travelling with two Inuit, also turned back. He never made it to the safety of the ship. He was shot by one of his Inuit companions because of his irrational behaviour, actions that they thought put their own safe return in jeopardy.

Finally, on April 1, Peary ordered Bob Bartlett, the Newfoundlander who was captain of the *Roosevelt*, to turn back. Bartlett did so reluctantly, but knew there was no choice. Peary had made it clear that he would not share the glory of reaching the North Pole with another white man. He would continue on with his Black assistant, Matthew Henson, and four Polar Inuit, Uutaaq, Ukkujaaq, Iggiannguaq, and Sigluk.

Peary and his party continued northward until April 6, when he announced that they had reached their destination; they remained there for about thirty hours. His diary entry for the following day was actually written some time later, while he was preparing his notes for publication. He wrote, "The Pole at last! The prize of 3 centuries, my dream and ambition for 23 years. Mine at last . . ."

Unlike modern polar adventurers, Peary and his party had no Twin Otters on call to pick them up and whisk them off to the accolades of well-wishers. Laboriously, they made the return journey back to Cape Columbia, which they reached on April 23, then on to the ship two days later.

Peary's claim has been disputed for the past century. His party of six included no one (including Peary) trained in navigation. Ironically, Bartlett, whom he had sent back to Cape Columbia, was a competent navigator and could have verified Peary's claims. But Bartlett also could have refuted them if, as many suspect, Peary had not reached the Pole. Suspicious too is the fact that once Bartlett had been sent back, Peary's claimed distances and speeds became incredible, almost three times what he had accomplished earlier. Peary described an almost straight-line dash to the Pole. This was contradicted by Matthew Henson's account of many detours to avoid open leads of water and pressure ridges of ice. Strange, too, was his behaviour on his return to the *Roosevelt*, iced in at Cape Columbia. He did not announce his achievement immediately, as one would expect of a man who had devoted so many years to the attainment of a single goal. When asked point-blank by Dr. Goodsell, Peary simply replied, "I have not been altogether unsuccessful." Modest words from a man never known for modesty.

The explorer Wally Herbert, who travelled to the Pole by dog sled, concluded that Peary missed his target by at least thirty miles. Close, but not close enough.

Peary's motto was, "I will find a way or make one." Even this was not original, having been appropriated from the Carthaginian military tactician Hannibal, who said, when faced with the task of crossing the Alps, "We will either find a way or make one." Given the scandal and controversy that have surrounded Robert Peary's dubious claims for a century, he might better have said, "I will find a way or fake one."

Peary was not able to get the news of his conquest of the Pole out to America for a number of months. His ship was securely frozen in and would not be released from the grip of the Arctic ice until summer. When word of his accomplishment finally reached the outside world in September, he would quickly learn that his rival, Dr. Frederick Cook, had just a few days earlier informed the world of his own attainment of the Pole in the spring of 1908, almost a year before Peary.

The accomplishments of these two men have been mired in controversy ever since. Cook claimed that there was glory enough for two. But that was easy for him to say, since he claimed to be first. As Peary knew, there really would be no praise and public glory for being second. And so the vicious denigration of Frederick Cook began. Today the debate continues among Polar scholars, writers, adventurers, and fanatics. It has lasted for over a century.

Ittukusuk, Aapilak, and Daagtikoorsuaq

Travels with Dr. Cook

F rederick Cook was born in New York State and educated as a doctor. But he was always drawn "Poleward" and often interrupted his medical practice to travel as a surgeon or leader on Arctic or Antarctic expeditions.

He first ventured into the Arctic as surgeon on Robert Peary's North Greenland Expedition in 1891. Although the two would later become bitter enemies, Peary praised the doctor at the time for his "unruffled patience and coolness in an emergency." Two other expeditions to Greenland and Labrador followed. As a result, a group of Americans interested in the North formed the Arctic Club of America. Frederick Cook was its first president, and was later president of the prestigious Explorers Club. After practicing medicine again and lecturing on his Northern experiences for four years, Cook joined the Belgian Antarctic expedition, where he was again praised for his courage.

In 1898 Peary returned north on an expedition that would last four years. Cook joined him in 1901, having been sent north on an errand of mercy. He found Peary to be "wrecked in ambition, wrecked in physique, and wrecked in hope." Cook attended to the man's health, and in the spring of 1902 Peary had recovered enough to make an attempt to reach the North Pole. It was unsuccessful, and Cook became convinced that Peary's so-called "American Route" to the Pole, north through Kane Basin, would never prove successful. After his return south, Cook directed his attention to other challenges, most notably Mount McKinley in Alaska, North America's highest peak. In 1906 he claimed to have reached its summit.

The following year Cook was drawn back to the High Arctic with a plan to reach the North Pole himself. He established a base camp at Anoritooq [Annoatok] on the Greenland coast of Kane Basin and passed the winter preparing to tackle exploration's greatest challenge. In February, accompanied by his German assistant and ten Inughuit, he crossed Ellesmere Island, skirted the east coast of Axel Heiberg Island, then headed north. He sent back his last supporting party after three days' travel over the sea ice. Accompanied only by two young Inughuit, Ittukusuk and Aapilak, he travelled on, and claimed to have reached the Pole on April 21, 1908. It was an anticlimax; he wrote: "The desolation . . . was such that it was almost palpable. . . . What a cheerless spot this was, to have aroused the ambition of man for so many years."

In Those Days

Robert Peary would claim the Pole almost a year later, on April 6, 1909, and the rivalry that would ensue would make Frederick Cook the most controversial and most maligned man in polar history. But all that was still a year away. First he had to return from the Pole to his base camp, and ultimately to the south.

Getting from Anoritooq to his farthest north—he claimed it was the Pole—had taken two months. Getting back would take a year. Heading south from his most northerly point, Cook misjudged the drift of the ice and ended up to the west of Axel Heiberg Island. Eventually he and his companions reached Jones Sound and spent the winter in a cave at Cape Sparbo on Devon Island, south of present-day Grise Fiord. The journey from there back to Greenland in the spring was made on foot, there being no dogs left. Dragging the remains of their sled behind them, surviving by chewing parts of their boots and leather ropes, they reached their base camp at Anoritooq in mid-April, the same time as Peary was returning to the *Roosevelt* from his farthest north.

Cook lost no time in heading south to announce his attainment of the Pole to an unsuspecting world. The *Roosevelt*, meanwhile, was still frozen in to her winter quarters and would be for some months.

In August, when Peary reached the Inuit village of Neqi, he first learned of the movements of Cook and his party. Even then he did not appear overly concerned. It was not until he called at Cape York on his final departure from the district that he became worried. There he picked up mail that had been cached for him by Captain Adams of the whaling ship *Morning*. In a letter marked "urgent," Adams informed Peary that Cook was in Upernavik, farther down the Greenland coast, claiming to have reached the Pole in 1908 and awaiting passage on the first ship south.

This news lit a fire under Peary. Now, after dallying in North Star Bay, he ordered Captain Bartlett to proceed at full speed for Indian Harbour, Labrador, the nearest telegraph station, fifteen hundred miles to the south.

Meanwhile, Frederick Cook was making his own way to a telegraph station. With an Inuk guide, Qulutannguaq, he had travelled by sled to Upernavik, south of Melville Bay, which he reached on May 21. He remained there for a month as guest of the Danish administrator. From there he continued on to Egedesminde, to await the arrival of another ship, which would take him to Copenhagen. Finally, on August 9, Cook departed Egedesminde aboard the *Hans Egede*. The captain of the vessel suggested that Cook get his news to the world as quickly as possible, and stopped at Lerwick in the Shetland Islands to allow him to do so. Early in the morning of September 1, the *Hans Egede* steamed up Bressay Sound, a boat was lowered, and Cook was rowed ashore. He sent three telegrams. The first, to George Lecointe, an old colleague from an earlier expedition, read simply: "Reached north pole April 21, 1908." The second was to his wife, Marie, in Brooklyn: "Successful and well. Wire address to Copenhagen." The third was a two-thousand-word message to a New York newspaper, the *Herald*. The next day the *Herald* published an article with a banner headline reading: "THE NORTH POLE IS DISCOVERED BY DR. FREDERICK A. COOK."

On September 6, while Cook was receiving the attention of the press and society in Copenhagen, Peary reached Indian Harbour telegraph station in Labrador and was finally able to announce his achievement to a world that was already lauding Cook. His first message was to his wife: "Have made good at last—I have the D.O.P." The initials stood for "damned old pole." Another message followed, to the secretary of the Peary Arctic Club: "Pole reached. Roosevelt safe. Peary." Other messages followed. One read, "Stars and Stripes Nailed to the Pole."

When Peary learned of Cook's prior claim, he cabled the *New York Times*: "Do not trouble about Cook's story. . . . He has not been to the Pole. . . . He has simply handed the public a gold brick."

For over two hundred years, men of different nations had sought the North Pole. Now two Americans were claiming it within five days. Cook had won the race to a telegraph station and was the first to claim to have reached the Pole.

But Peary had wealth and influence backing him. Ten years earlier, powerful supporters had formed the Peary Arctic Club to assist him in his quest. Now, the club went into action against the upstart surgeon from New York. A concerted campaign of vilification and lies ruined Cook's credibility. Eventually he entered the oil business in Texas. But even there he was hounded by his old enemies. Convicted on trumped-up charges of fraud in the promotion of his business, Cook was sentenced in 1923 to fourteen years in Leavenworth Penitentiary. Even in 1930, when he became eligible for parole, Professor William Hobbs, a biographer of Peary, organized a protest against his release. The protest failed and Cook was freed. In 1940, shortly before his death, he received a pardon from President Roosevelt. Frederick Cook died on August 5, 1940. He was seventy-five.

Calling Frederick Cook "upright, honorable, capable and conscientious in the extreme," Roald Amundsen, the first man to reach the South Pole, also said of him: "We shall always honor Dr. Frederick A. Cook as the first man at the geographical North Pole of the earth. It was a pity that Peary should besmirch his beautiful work by circulating outrageous accusations against a competitor who has won the battle in open field."

Most scholars today doubt that either man reached the North Pole. Most Inughuit believe that Cook lied about his claim. This is all the more unusual because they remember him with kindly feelings. One reason for this favourable view is his command of their language, Inuktun. It takes time, and a close engagement with people, to develop facility in a language. And so it is noteworthy that Inuutersuaq Ulloriaq, the late historian of the Inughuit, wrote, "Daagtikoorsuaq [the Polar Eskimo name for Dr. Cook] had a remarkable command of the polar Eskimo language." At the same time he wrote, "I know that later they [Ittukusuk and Aapilak] were interrogated very thoroughly about the North Pole, by Piulersuaq [a variant of Piulirriaq, Peary] himself. They of course admitted that he had lied. I am in no doubt either that Daagtikoorsuaq never let the two young men, Aapilak and Itukusuk [sic], know anything of his lie about them reaching the North Pole. He was able to do this because they did not know where the North Pole lay, or so he thought then."

* * *

In the spring of 1909 Frederick Cook and his two Inuit companions, Ittukusuk and Aapilak, struggled along the coast of Ellesmere Island, heading in a general northeasterly direction towards Greenland, after spending the winter in a cave on northern Devon Island. Near the Ellesmere coast, the party discovered

In Those Days

two small, high islands at 76°13'00" north latitude, 79°51'00" west longitude.

Cook describes that part of the journey thus:

> At the end of eight days of forced marches we reached Cape Tennyson. The disadvantage of manpower, when compared to dog motive force, was clearly shown in this effort. The ice was free of pressure troubles and the weather was endurable. Still, with the best of luck, we had averaged only about seven miles daily. With dogs, the entire run would have been made easily in two days.
>
> As we neared the land two small islands were discovered. Both were about one thousand feet high, with precipitous sea walls, and were on a line about two miles east of Cape Tennyson. The most easterly was about one and a half miles long, east to west, with a cross-section, north to south, of about three-quarters of a mile. About half a mile to the west of this was a much smaller island. There was no visible vegetation, and no life was seen, although hare and fox tracks were crossed on the ice.[27]

Cook decided to permanently memorialize his two travelling companions by naming the islands after them. Like almost all explorers, his rendering of Inuktitut names was idiosyncratic. In his own words, he tells us that "I decided to call the larger island E-tuk-i-shook, and the smaller Ah-we-lah." Those words were published in 1911. Forty years later, in his posthumously published *Return from the Pole*, only one line was changed. Cook wrote that

---

[27] Dr. Frederick A. Cook, *My Attainment of the Pole* (New York: Polar Publishing Company, 1911), 427.

he had decided to call the larger island Etuq and the smaller Wela. These abbreviations were his nicknames for the two young men with whom he travelled.

Unfortunately, the two names in either their full or abbreviated versions never made it onto the official map of Canada.

Records are sparse, but the two islands were officially named the Stewart Islands, after the Honourable Charles Stewart and his wife Lady Jane Stewart. Strangely enough, official records do not show one island as named for Charles Stewart and the other for his wife, but rather both islands being collectively named the Stewart Islands after both of them. Probably the islands were named during an official Canadian government expedition to the High Arctic in 1922 under the command of John Davidson Craig aboard the vessel *Arctic*, under the captaincy of Joseph-Elzéar Bernier. The naming probably occurred when the vessel went north from Pond Inlet to establish the RCMP post at nearby Craig Harbour. Charles Stewart had been appointed federal minister of the interior and mines the previous year.

Neither Charles Stewart nor his wife ever visited the Canadian Arctic, so never set eyes on the two islands named for them. Ittukusuk and Aapilak did, in the spring of 1909. In light of this, and in view of the need to commemorate meaningful Inuit participation in Arctic exploration, it is high time that the names Ittukusuk (for the larger island) and Aapilak (for the smaller) officially replace the designation Stewart Islands. Ittukusuk and Aapilak deserve their islands.

"The Trail That Is Always New"

Matthew Henson and His Inuit Family

Robert Peary probably did not reach the North Pole on April 6, 1909. Unfortunately, that means that neither did Matthew Henson, his Black sledge-mate, or the four Inuit who accompanied them on their final dash from the point where Bob Bartlett had been sent back.

That's too bad, because no one deserved the honour of reaching the highest latitude on earth more than Henson. In recent years, many Black historians and writers have fought long and hard to have Henson recognized as co-discoverer of the North Pole. Some have even suggested that Henson was the first person to set foot on the Pole, because he would have been out in front of Peary's sled, breaking trail, while the ostensible leader, virtually an invalid, rode on a sled. Henson wrote, "I, who had walked, knew that we had made exceptional distance. . . . So did the Eskimos, for they also had walked. Lieutenant Peary . . . because of his crippled feet, had ridden on the sledge the greater part of the journey up."

Matthew Henson was born in 1866 in Maryland. Orphaned at thirteen, he went to sea the same year and was fortunate to attract the attentions of the captain, a white man who recognized the boy's innate intelligence and taught him reading, writing, and navigation. At the age of twenty-one, working in Washington, DC, Henson met Robert Peary, then a young naval lieutenant, and agreed to accompany him on a surveying expedition to Nicaragua. This was the start of Henson's long association with Peary. In 1891 he accompanied Peary to northwestern Greenland on an expedition that was the first of many and that would culminate in Peary's "assault" on the Pole in 1909.

Peary believed in the supremacy of the white race. He believed that Henson and the Inuit were inferior to him. On one occasion he berated Henson for not calling him "Sir" often enough. He also wrote that Henson was "as subject to my will as the fingers of my hand." He even had the audacity to say that the reason he sent Bartlett, an accomplished navigator, back before the final dash to the Pole, instead of sending Henson back, was because he didn't think that Henson could face the responsibility of returning to the ship alone. In his own words: "He had not, as a racial inheritance, the daring and initiative of Bartlett, or Marvin, or MacMillan, or Borup. I owed it to him not to subject him to dangers and responsibilities which he was temperamentally unfit to face."

In Those Days

Chief among the Henson advocates have been the late Dr. Alan Counter, a professor of neurology at Harvard Medical School, and Verne Robinson, son of Henson's earliest biographer, Bradley Robinson, who published *Dark Companion* in 1947. Both have done admirable jobs of advancing Henson's cause, but unfortunately Henson's claim rests on Peary's claim, and Peary's claim is suspect, unproven, and increasingly unbelieved. The Henson claim is simply this: because Peary reached the Pole, Henson must have reached it first.

It's also ironic that these Black writers who champion Henson as being first at the Pole must also be tacit supporters of Peary, the racist who downplayed Henson's abilities. Some claim that there was an unspoken bond of friendship and respect between the two men. Perhaps Henson felt that way about Peary. But the feeling was not reciprocated. It is wishful thinking, not supported by the evidence.

On the return from their farthest north, Peary hardly spoke to Henson. Henson wrote, "From the time we were at the Pole Commander Peary scarcely spoke to me. Probably he did not speak to me four times on the whole return journey to the ship. I thought this over and it grieved me much. I thought of the years we had worked together for the one great aim. . . . It nearly broke my heart on the return journey from the Pole that he would rise in the morning and slip away on the homeward trail without rapping on the ice for me, as was the established custom."

But if Matthew Henson cannot be remembered as the discoverer or co-discoverer of the Pole, how should he be remembered? I suggest that Matthew Henson was one of the greatest travellers to ever set foot in the Arctic, a man who lived with the Inuit on their terms and learned from them. He learned their methods of travel—he is remembered as an excellent dog driver—and he learned their language better than any other explorer. The Inuit of northern Greenland loved and admired him. They gave him a name, Maripaluk, and it is by this name that he is remembered with respect to this day. Whatever farthest north Peary achieved, it was Henson who took him there, and back. Without Henson, Peary was nothing.

Henson had one child in Greenland, the product of his loving relationship with an Inuit woman, Aqattannguaq. That son was Anaukkaq, whom I knew well in the 1970s. When I first met him he was an elderly man with an insatiable curiosity about his father, the legendary Maripaluk. He asked what I knew of him and whether he had had any children in the south.

What I learned was the long and sad conclusion of the life of the legendary explorer. The glory was all for Peary. Henson found a job as a parking lot attendant in Brooklyn, and later as a messenger boy at the US Customs House in New York City. Eventually it dawned on a changing world that this man was a hero. In 1945 he received a medal for his work on Peary's expedition. In 1954 President Eisenhower received Henson and his wife, Lucy, at the White House.

After Henson left the Arctic for good in 1909, Anaukkaq was raised by Aqattannguaq and her husband, Qillaq. He married Aviaq, and they had six sons and numerous grandchildren. One of those grandchildren is also named Aviaq Henson. She lives in Nuuk and is a devoted student of Matthew Henson and his legacy. She suggested to the Greenland postal authorities that they issue a stamp commemorating Matthew Henson. (In 2005 they had issued a Peary stamp.) The postal authorities agreed, and a stamp honouring Matthew Henson was issued in 2009

In Those Days

on Greenland's National Day, June 21. In addition to a flattering image of Henson, the first day cover also featured an image of a smiling Aqattannguaq carrying her baby in a traditional *amaut* on her back. (In 1986 Henson and Peary were jointly featured on an American commemorative stamp.)

A year after Henson was received at the White House, he died of a cerebral hemorrhage at the age of eighty-eight. In 1988, in death, he was again honoured by the nation he had served. His body was disinterred from his grave in the Bronx and reburied, with full honours, in Arlington National Cemetery, the resting place of America's heroes, where Peary's body had lain since 1920. On his tombstone are inscribed his own words: "The lure of the Arctic is tugging at my heart. To me the trail is calling. The old trail. The trail that is always new."

Through the efforts of Dr. Alan Counter, his champion, a number of Henson's Inuit descendants from Greenland were brought to Arlington for the burial ceremony. Among them was Maripaluk's aged son Anaukkaq. At his father's graveside, he spoke about the importance this ceremony had for him. Since he was a young boy, he had been curious to know more of his father. His dreams had now been fulfilled. He was an old man, he said, and sick. Now he could return to his Arctic village and die in peace. Anaukkaq returned to Greenland, contented, and died a month later.

Inughuit and the Myth of Crocker Land

In 1906, Robert Peary was travelling with a small party of Inuit from northwestern Greenland southward along the west coast of what he called Grant Land, what we today know as Ellesmere Island. He and his companions climbed to two thousand feet elevation at one point, to survey the land and sea ahead of them. To their west lay the ice of Nansen Strait, still solid in late June. And beyond it lay the land Peary called Jesup's Land, today known as Axel Heiberg Island.

And northwest? Something else interested him, something he claimed his Inuit assistants had referred to a few days earlier:

"North stretched the well-known ragged surface of the polar pack, and northwest it was with a thrill that my glasses revealed the faint white summits of a distant land which my Eskimos claimed to have seen as we came along from the last camp."

Peary crossed Nansen Strait to Axel Heiberg Island and reached a point at the western mouth of a small bay, a point that he named Cape Thomas Hubbard, after one of his major benefactors who also served as president of the Peary Arctic Club.

On June 28 he and his Inuit companions climbed to the summit of the cape, and Peary later wrote:

> The clear day greatly favoured my work in taking a round of angles, and with the glasses I could make out apparently a little more distinctly, the snow-clad summits of the distant land in the north-west, above the ice horizon.
>
> My heart leaped the intervening miles of ice as I looked longingly at this land, and in fancy I trod its shores and climbed its summits, even though I knew that that pleasure could be only for another in another season.[28]

Peary named this far-off discovery Crocker Land, after another benefactor, George Crocker. Strangely, though, the name does not appear in the text of his book about this expedition, *Nearest the Pole*, although it does appear on the accompanying map. He estimated the land to be 130 miles away at about 83° north and 100° west.

Peary's quotation indicates that he knew he would never set foot on Crocker Land—he was focused on only one goal, and that was the North Pole. But the possibility of this unknown land in

---

[28] Robert E. Peary, *Nearest the Pole: A Narrative of the Polar Expedition of the Peary Arctic Club in the S. S. Roosevelt, 1905-1906* (New York: Doubleday, Page and Co., 1907), 207.

the Arctic Ocean beckoned other explorers. In 1913 Vilhjalmur Stefansson arrived in the western Arctic on his second Arctic venture, the Canadian Arctic Expedition. One of his goals was to search the Beaufort Sea and beyond for any signs of land, including Crocker Land. By mid-1915 Stefansson was certain that Peary's Crocker Land had been an illusion.

* * *

When Peary claimed to have reached the North Pole in April 1909, it marked the end of his Arctic career. But for one young man who had accompanied him north, it was the first of many Arctic adventures. That man was Donald Baxter MacMillan. He would return to the far North in 1913, obsessed with finding the land that Peary had claimed to have seen in 1906.

Three years after his alleged attainment of the Pole, Peary still believed, or claimed to believe, in his discovery. He wrote, "Crocker Land easily takes first rank among problems demanding exploration, now that the Poles have been reached and that the insularity of Greenland has been determined."

The following year, his young acolyte, MacMillan, rose to the challenge. He organized the Crocker Land Expedition, a four-year affair sponsored by the American Museum of Natural History, the American Geographical Society, and the University of Illinois.

From the base he established at Etah (Iita), near the point where Greenland and Ellesmere Island are at their closest, MacMillan and his parties explored northern Ellesmere Island, the coasts of Axel Heiberg Island, and as far west as King Christian and Ellef Ringnes islands.

173

In Those Days

But MacMillan had a problem that he had not anticipated. He had assumed that, because he had been with Peary and Henson, to whom the Inughuit had shown intense personal loyalty as a result of eighteen years of association, the Inughuit would automatically transfer their loyalty to him. He was mistaken. He could not command the authority of Peary. And, although he had brought quantities of trade goods with him, the Danes Knud Rasmussen and Peter Freuchen were now operating their Thule Station, a trading post at North Star Bay, so the Inughuit had an alternative source of goods. The older, more experienced and influential Inughuit did not give MacMillan the deference and unquestioning loyalty he demanded. They questioned his judgment and his decisions. As a result, he fired many of them, deciding to make the difficult trip across Ellesmere Island and onto the ice of the Arctic Ocean with a mix of experienced and inexperienced travellers.

On March 10, 1914, MacMillan, two white men, and six Inughuit left Etah in search of Crocker Land. The first and most difficult task was to mount the almost perpendicular face of the Beitstad Glacier on Ellesmere Island. With that accomplished, they sledged north to Cape Thomas Hubbard, the point on which Peary had stood eight years earlier when he surveyed the horizon and first caught sight of Crocker Land. By the time the party reached that point, five men had been sent back or had turned back. The party was down to four men: MacMillan; Fitzhugh Green, an American; Ittukusuk, who had travelled in these very parts with Dr. Frederick Cook in 1907–08; and Piugaattoq, a respected hunter and traveller who was married to the woman who had been Peary's long-time lover.

The Inughuit were reluctant to travel out onto the sea ice north of Axel Heiberg. The season was late and there was much open water. But MacMillan badgered them into continuing, and in doing so endangered the lives of all of the party. Finally, on April 21, Fitzhugh Green sighted Crocker Land. "There it was as plain as day," wrote MacMillan, "hills, valleys, and ice cap—a tremendous land extending through 150 degrees of the horizon."

MacMillan was ecstatic. His name would be famous forever for confirming the existence of this new land to the north. "It could even be seen without a glass," he wrote, adding, "Our powerful glasses, however . . . brought out more clearly the dark background in contrast with the white." He asked Piugaattoq for advice on the best route through the ice to reach the new discovery. To his astonishment, the Inuk replied that there was no land, only "poo-jok"—mist. MacMillan didn't believe him. But after studying the horizon for some time more, MacMillan had to concede, "As we watched it more narrowly its appearance slowly changed from time to time so we were forced to the conclusion that it was a mirage of the sea ice."

But the next day, not wanting to admit defeat, the foolhardy MacMillan insisted on proceeding further. The Inughuit reluctantly agreed. For another few days they chased the mirage over increasingly dangerous sea ice. Finally Fitzhugh Green calculated that the point on which they stood should be Crocker Land. As they were standing on sea ice with no land in sight, the conclusion was now beyond doubt: Crocker Land did not exist. MacMillan wrote, "My dreams of the last four years were merely dreams, my hopes had ended in bitter disappointment."

MacMillan, as Peary before him, had been deceived by a mirage, a trick played on him by the atmospheric conditions of an Arctic spring and the vagaries of shifting sea ice. Crocker Land was nothing more than ice and snow, reflected and refracted through the lens of an Arctic mist.

Getting Away
with Murder

Safely back on Axel Heiberg Island after chasing the mists that were Crocker Land, MacMillan felt a need to salvage something from his journey. He decided to travel to a cape on Ellesmere Island with Ittukusuk as guide, to retrieve a record left there by the Norwegian explorer Otto Sverdrup. He instructed expedition member Fitzhugh Green to travel westward with the other hunter, Piugaattoq, to further explore the coast of Axel Heiberg. But Piugaattoq objected because a storm was brewing. Nevertheless, MacMillan ordered them to leave at once. Piugaattoq reluctantly obeyed.

When the storm hit, Piugaattoq dug a shelter for the two men in a snowbank. Then a snowslide buried Green's sled and killed his dogs. Desperately, Piugaattoq worked to keep a pocket of air open in the cavern he had hollowed out for himself and Green.

The American was "green" in more than name, but Piugaattoq persevered, and kept him alive.

When the storm abated, Piugaattoq announced that they must return to rendezvous with MacMillan. But Green, despite his inexperience, wanted to continue. The two men argued. A second storm forced them back into the close confines of their refuge.

Finally Piugaattoq had had enough. He told Green that to proceed was foolish and that he was turning back. They had only one sled between them, and Piugaattoq forced Green to walk, knowing that the activity was necessary to keep his toes from freezing. Green complained that he could not keep up, but Piugaattoq maintained a steady pace.

Green may have felt that Piugaattoq was abandoning him. On the march, he snatched a rifle from the sled and brandished it in Piugaattoq's direction, ordering the Inuk to follow behind him. When he turned a few minutes later, he saw a frightened Piugaattoq whipping the dogs frantically off in another direction.

Green reported what happened next matter-of-factly in his journal: "I shot once in the air. He did not stop. I then killed him with a shot through the shoulder and another through the head."

Piugaattoq had been a trusted travel companion of Robert Peary on his polar expeditions. The explorer and anthropologist Knud Rasmussen described him as "a man whom one could trust" and "a comrade who in difficult or dangerous circumstances was ready to make personal sacrifices in order to help and support his companions." Piugaattoq had tried to save Green's life. Green had taken his.

Green returned alone to the expedition's headquarters at Etah. On May 4, 1914, MacMillan recorded the death of Piugaattoq in his diary, as told to him by Green:

In Those Days

Twice I found Pee-ah-wah-to trying to get away from me by leaving the trail. Watching my chance I quickly grabbed the rifle from the sledge, I asked him where the igloo was. Starting out in the direction of his pointed arm I ordered him to follow closely behind me. Looking back a few minutes later I noticed that he had left the trail again. I shot over his head. He did not stop so I shot him through the body. He fell back against the upstanders. As the dogs did not stop I thought that possibly he might still be alive so I shot again splitting his head open so that his brains fell out.[29]

Back in America, MacMillan published his story of the Crocker Land Expedition four years later, and wrote dispassionately that "Green, inexperienced in the handling of Eskimos, and failing to understand their motives and temperament, had felt it necessary to shoot his companion."

At Etah, MacMillan and Green determined to keep the truth from the Inughuit. They told them a half-truth instead. There had been a snowslide, they said, and Piugaattoq had suffocated under it. But Ittukusuk knew what had happened as soon as Green returned to MacMillan's camp. He had been around Americans long enough that he knew a little English, and he had heard the distraught Green blurt out his dismal tale to MacMillan. Ittukusuk told the other Inughuit the truth when they returned to the expedition's headquarters. The Inughuit decided not to let on that any of them knew.

Green's actions defy logic. If a man felt he was being abandoned by his guide in unfamiliar and dangerous territory, why shoot the

---

[29] Crocker Land Expedition: Donald MacMillan Journal Extract, Box 2, Folder 7 (May 4, 1914); in Fitzhugh Green, Sr., Papers, Lauinger Library, Georgetown University, Washington, DC.

guide? That would simply lessen one's chance of survival. The story makes no sense. Unless there was more to it.

Many of the Inughuit thought that, indeed, there was another reason. Many years ago, when I asked the elders in Qaanaaq why they thought Fitzhugh Green had killed Piugaattoq, they told me that the reason was simple—Green had wanted Piugaattoq's wife, Aleqasina. She was a strikingly beautiful woman who had been Peary's mistress until he abandoned her in 1909. Green, the Inughuit believed, desired her. To them, no other reason could explain such an irrational act.

Although MacMillan wrote about it, the murder of Piugaattoq was never investigated. Fitzhugh Green was never punished.

Sovereignty 101

Captain Joseph-Elzéar Bernier and the Inuit

Captain Joseph-Elzéar Bernier had a long and illustrious association with the Canadian Arctic. Inuit remember him as Kapitaikallak—the stocky captain. He was a physically impressive man. A contemporary described him, in advancing years, as being "below medium height but massive, with a bull neck and muscular arms and shoulders. Though overweight, he was nimble and sturdy. . . . His head was bald on top, fringed by white hair, and he had a matching walrus moustache. His mouth was large and contained an array of gold bridgework. His nose was bulbous, his chin was heavy and his face was broad and florid. His eyes were keen. He wore glasses only for reading."

Bernier was born in the French-speaking village of L'Islet in Quebec on the southern shores of the St. Lawrence River on New Year's Day, 1852. It would have been surprising had he not turned to the sea, for saltwater had coursed through his family's veins for three generations. He made his first sea voyage as a baby of two years and became captain of a vessel at seventeen. He would be at sea, save for a few brief intervals, for sixty years, and would command over one hundred ships. He crossed the Atlantic more than five hundred times.

In 1871 Bernier saw the *Polaris* in drydock being readied for a voyage north in which the American explorer Charles Francis Hall hoped to reach the North Pole. This chance observance aroused his interest in the Arctic, and he later wrote that the experience "led me to read up the history of polar exploration in my spare time, and to study assiduously the problems of Arctic navigation. From 1872 my cabin library on shipboard consisted mainly of books on Arctic travel, and the latest Arctic maps were always in my chartroom."

Not until 1896, however, during a period of temporary retirement from the sea, did Bernier have the leisure to turn his thoughts seriously northward. The previous year he had received a prestigious appointment as governor of the Quebec City jail, a position he would hold for three years. This sinecure allowed him the free time to study the challenges and potential of the Arctic, and he set for himself an ambitious goal. He would discover the North Pole for Canada.

To be the first to reach the geographical point where all lines of longitude meet had been a goal of explorers and adventurers for almost as long as the Northwest Passage had occupied their attentions. Already Robert Peary was active in prosecuting his attempts on the Pole from a land base in northwestern Greenland and would shortly begin to use bases in Ellesmere Island, nominally Canadian territory. Bernier felt strongly that the glory of polar discovery should be Canada's. "And why should Canada not reap the benefits of all the work accomplished so far?" he asked the Quebec Geographical Society in 1898. "Why should we allow other countries to overtake us?. . . . Why should Canadians not go as far north as ninety degrees and place their flag on that part of the globe, the northernmost boundary of Canada, a country that is part of the British Empire?"

These are words that should resonate to the embarrassment of all Canadians, especially now, over a hundred years later, as our nation continues to struggle with its Northern vision.

Bernier was an able publicist. His country had yet to have anyone champion the cause of the Arctic and preach the necessity of exerting its sovereignty in a territory largely the domain of foreign whalers and explorers. With flair and skill, he began to promote his dream of conquering the Pole, preparing detailed plans for achieving his goal. But although he won the support of many influential politicians, he failed to get sufficient financial backing to mount a private expedition. He turned, therefore, to the government, hoping to organize an official voyage on its behalf. The government's reaction was unusual. While never firmly committing itself to support a Bernier-led polar expedition, it did nonetheless give him permission to select and purchase for the government a ship suitable for Arctic work. Bernier naturally assumed the ship would be used for his Northern venture.

In 1904 he went to Germany and purchased the *Gauss*, a ship built there three years earlier for an expedition that had wintered successfully in the Antarctic. Back in Canada and renamed the

Arctic, the vessel was provisioned with supplies sufficient for three years for Bernier's attempt on the Pole. But in July, shortly before the *Arctic* was due to leave, the prime minister, Sir Wilfrid Laurier, announced a change in plans—the *Arctic* would go instead to Hudson Bay to deliver supplies to the Royal North-West Mounted Police post established the previous year at Fullerton. The government had learned that American whalers were fishing the northern waters of Canada's vast inland sea and feared for the validity of its claimed sovereignty over the area.

Bernier was bitterly disappointed. For years he had planned and publicized his vision of Canada at the Pole and, at the last possible moment, the opportunity had been snatched from him. True, he was to act as captain of the ship, and it was a voyage to the Arctic, but this was little consolation; another man, Superintendent J. D. Moodie of the Royal North-West Mounted Police, had been given command of the expedition itself.

In the summer of 1904, Bernier took the *Arctic* to Hudson Bay, where he delivered supplies to the Fullerton post, a one-storey wooden structure, twenty-five feet by fifteen. He wintered his vessel there, just four hundred yards from the post and only two hundred yards from the American whaler the *Era*, under Captain George Comer, one of the perceived threats to Canadian sovereignty. The *Arctic* returned to Quebec the following October. The wintering had served only to bolster Bernier's fascination with the Arctic. It also introduced him to the Inuit, with whom he had a positive relationship. He vowed that he would return, but it was the High Arctic that he longed for.

* * *

In Those Days

Back in southern Canada in the fall of 1905, Bernier immediately began talking up his North Pole hopes again. But Ottawa had different duties in mind for this energetic French-Canadian patriot.

In 1906 the Department of Marine and Fisheries gave him a new assignment: to organize a voyage to the Arctic Archipelago to formally annex all new lands at which he called, to leave proclamations in cairns at all points, and to collect customs dues from foreign whaling ships working Canadian waters. Bernier, fifty-four years old at the time, acknowledged the end of his polar ambitions when he wrote, "I determined to devote my efforts . . . to what after all may be regarded as a more important object, that is to say to securing all the islands in the Arctic archipelago for Canada. . . . I regarded this work of greater importance than any attempts to reach the pole so far as Canada was concerned."

Once in the North, Bernier pushed the *Arctic* into Lancaster Sound, then around Bylot Island's northern coast, then south and east to the Scottish whaling station at Albert Harbour. There he learned that no whalers had been seen yet that year. Retracing his route northward, Bernier forced his ship through Barrow Strait, formally taking possession for Canada of many islands in the Arctic Archipelago. He reached his farthest west at Melville Island.

Bernier felt passionately that the people who lived on the land he claimed must be made to realize that their land had been alienated and that they were Canadian citizens. He realized, too, that he would need their assistance in achieving his goals. For his journey west to Melville Island, he hired two Inuit men, one old and one young, to accompany him. They were Miqqusaaq and Qamaniq. He described his purpose in taking them along: "I wanted them to tell their friends what they had seen to the west. If I had taken only a young man, his story would not have been accepted unreservedly by his tribesmen, but with corroboration by an older man his statements would be unquestioned. . . . I also wanted them to get acquainted with government officials and to get used to the notion that they were now wards of the government, and must accordingly begin to adopt the ways of white men, especially in observing the laws of the country."

The process of acculturation of the Inuit of the High Arctic had formally begun. Bernier's official orders make no reference to the Inuit, only to land. The government had not yet realized that effective sovereignty over an isolated territory required something more than the erecting of cairns and the reading of proclamations. More prescient than the bureaucrats in far-off Ottawa, Bernier himself had taken the initiative to explain the ways of his country to the Inuit. He would raise cairns and read proclamations at almost every landfall, as required, but he had also determined that only through informing the Inuit of what he was doing could he establish a meaningful sovereignty over this vast Arctic territory.

Bernier returned to Albert Harbour and began making plans to winter. On Christmas Day, he hosted about 120 Inuit for a festive dinner aboard ship, afterwards giving them a lecture on good citizenship. On the king's birthday a royal salute was fired, and Bernier took official possession of Baffin Island. He reported, "A speech was made to the men and the natives, by myself; calling [to] the attention of the natives that they had become Canadians, and that we expected them to live in peace and respect one another, and conform themselves to the laws of the Government of the Dominion of Canada."

The *Arctic* broke free from her winter quarters and headed for open sea on July 27. Bernier collected whaling licence fees from Captain Cooney of the Scottish ship *Morning* and explored the entrance to Jones Sound, claiming more land for Canada, before returning to Quebec City in mid-October.

The Inuit of northern Baffin Island had had their first taste of white officialdom; under Bernier's beneficent approach, it had not been unpleasant.

* * *

In 1908 Ottawa sent Bernier to the High Arctic again. That expedition wintered on Melville Island at Winter Harbour, far north of where any Inuit lived. There, on July 1, 1909, he proclaimed sovereignty over the entire Arctic Archipelago as far north as the Pole, the first time Canada had claimed ownership based on the sector principle, which divided the far North into pie-shaped slices, with the Pole at the centre.

Bernier was ordered north on yet another High Arctic expedition in 1910, this time to patrol the waters surrounding the Arctic Islands, attempt the Northwest Passage, issue whaling licenses to foreign whalers, and act as Justice of the Peace and protector of wildlife. But this would be a voyage very different from his two previous excursions into the High Arctic. This voyage would lead to controversy, and ultimately to Bernier's resignation from government service.

As early as 1909, he had written privately to the Department of the Interior, filing several applications for land in the Pond Inlet area (the body of water separating Baffin and Bylot islands) and stating, "I beg to be allowed the honour to be one of the first Canadian settlers on the Arctic Archipelago." On April 5, 1910, he purchased the whaling station at "Pond's Bay" and the storehouse and equipment at Button Point on Bylot Island from Robert Kinnes of Dundee, Scotland. Six weeks later, on May 16, the Department of the Interior granted him a tract of land 960 acres in area on the south side of "Pond's Inlet." The government knew very well that Bernier was a civil servant who had been paid handsomely for his services to the government on his previous expeditions, and that he was "proceeding again to the Arctic regions during the present year." Nonetheless, they granted him this huge tract of land "in recognition of the grantee's services in connection with the said Arctic expeditions." Immodestly, Bernier named his land Berniera.

When he departed later that summer on his official voyage to the High Arctic, Bernier was, unknown to his crew members, the only private landowner in Baffin Island. The voyage of 1910–11, which wintered at Arctic Bay, would end in acrimony. Bernier, it was later alleged, was trading government-owned supplies to the Inuit for his own personal benefit and profit. On his return south, he resigned from government service, purchased his own small schooner, and became a private trader.

After some years in private trade, Bernier sold his Arctic holdings to a rival and retired. But a few years later, he was called back into government service to serve again as captain of his old vessel, the *Arctic*, for some years. He died in 1934.

The Inuit were oblivious to the passions that drove a man like Bernier. But it was their land that he coveted on behalf of a largely disinterested nation, and for himself. With no previous understanding of formalized government, in fact no background against which to consider Bernier's words, it is doubtful whether the Inuit understood many of the concepts that Bernier was trying to convey to them in the lectures on being a Canadian that he periodically delivered. But these first lessons in civics were as good as any that they were to hear for many more decades.

"We're Going to Keep On Living"
Ruth Makpii Ipalook on Stefansson's Karluk Expedition

In 1913 the Canadian government sponsored an expedition to the western Canadian Arctic—today's Kitikmeot Region— to carry out scientific work and geographical exploration. It was led by Vilhjalmur Stefansson, a Canadian of Icelandic origin, who would end up with a reputation seriously tarnished by the results of the expedition.

Stefansson himself commanded the expedition's Northern Division, the one that would have exploration as its main objective. His ship, the *Karluk*, was built as a fishing vessel for California and was never meant for the Arctic ice. But she was commanded by a veteran Newfoundland captain, Bob Bartlett, a man with considerable Arctic experience, which included his command of the *Roosevelt* on Peary's final polar expedition. She sailed from Victoria in July. The party had planned to winter at Banks Island, but ice prevented the ship from reaching its destination. Instead, the vessel spent the winter locked in the icy grip of the Beaufort Sea. This was, in fact, Stefansson's own fault, for the departure of the ship from Victoria had been delayed while he continued to raise money.

Stefansson was one of the few Qallunaat onboard who knew how to hunt. In September, he left the ship, taking with him five men—including two Alaskan Inuit—on what he said would be a hunting expedition to the Alaskan mainland. In fact, he made no attempt to return to the *Karluk*; he and his party wintered with the expedition's other two ships at Collinson Point. Stefansson subsequently claimed that he had tried to return to the ship, but critics forever after accused him of abandoning the ship and its crew, and bearing personal responsibility for the tragedy that ensued.

While Stefansson wintered in relative comfort, the *Karluk* drifted slowly westward towards Siberia for three months in the dead of winter, at the mercy of the wind, weather, and cold. On January 10, in the darkest part of winter, the crew was awakened by a harsh grating sound. A crack had opened along the starboard length of the ship, and she was taking on water. That evening, realizing that the situation was hopeless, Captain Bartlett gave orders to abandon ship. The crew, the scientific staff, and the Inuit took refuge on the ice, where they had already constructed a makeshift house of boxes and barrels for the Qallunaat and an attached snow house for the Inuit.

Most of the men had no Arctic experience, but they were assisted by two Inuit, Kurraluk and Kataktovik. Both men were excellent hunters and had kept the expedition supplied with fresh seal meat during the westward drift. Earlier in the expedition, when the *Karluk* had stopped at Barrow, Alaska, Stefansson had recruited the two men as hunters to keep the expedition supplied with food throughout the winter, which they expected to spend on uninhabited Banks Island. One hunter, Kurraluk, had been recommended above all others. He was willing to go, but he insisted on taking his wife and two children. So his wife, Qiruk, and two little girls, eight-year-old Qaġġualuk (later known as Helen) and little Makpii (later known as Ruth), went along. Qiruk—whom all the crew came to know as "Auntie"—would be busy; in addition to looking after her two children, she was seamstress, sewing skin clothing for twenty-seven men.

With his ship slowly succumbing to the pressures of the ice, Captain Bartlett remained aboard that night, clearly distraught at the impending loss of a vessel under his command. William Laird McKinlay, a diminutive Scottish mathematics teacher who had signed on as meteorologist and magnetician, described that night:

> He had a huge fire roaring in the galley stove, and he had moved the gramophone in with the full stock of records. He played them one by one, throwing each record as it ended into the galley fire. He found Chopin's Funeral March, played it over and laid it aside. He was really very comfortable, eating when he felt like it and drinking plenty of coffee and tea. There was just enough ice pressure to keep the ship from sinking. . . . All day the Captain remained on board. For hours nothing changed. The ship was full of water and only prevented from sinking by the grip of the ice. . . . Then at 3:15 a shout, "She's going!" brought everyone on to the ice. The

Karluk was settling down at the bow. As the minutes went by, the deck sank almost entirely under water. Captain Bartlett put the Funeral March on the Victrola. With the water running along the starboard side of the deck and pouring down the hatches, he waited at the rail until it came down level with the ice. Then he stepped off. The *Karluk* slowly settled by the bow and sank gradually. . . . Captain Bartlett, deeply moved, stood right alongside her until she was gone.[30]

The worst was yet to come. When Stefansson had abandoned the party, he had taken twelve of the best dogs with him. Now, with poor dogs, the remains of the Northern Division set out over the ice for Wrangel Island, north of Siberia. Bartlett knew that their only hope of survival was to reach the uninhabited island. The *Karluk*'s first officer, Sandy Anderson, only twenty years old, was the first to die. An indication of the severity of the conditions is evident from the fact that two of the others who died early in the attempt to reach the island were two men who had been with Shackleton in the Antarctic in 1909, and who had crossed the land ice near the South Pole. In all, eight men died on the ice of the Arctic Ocean.

On the desperate journey over the ice, Kurraluk's daughter, little Makpii, almost perished. Years later, her daughter, Emily Wilson, recounted the tale that has been passed down in the family. "One night as the tired party slept fully clothed in case of emergency," she said, "my grandmother heard the sudden cracking of the ice and then saw the ice crack right under my mother. There wasn't even time to grab her. She just pushed her right to the

---

[30] William Laird McKinley, *Karluk: The Great Untold Story of Arctic Exploration* (London: Weidenfeld and Nicolson, 1976), 67–68.

other side of the crack, and that saved her life. Otherwise my mother would have fallen into the sea right there."

Makpii was remembered throughout her life for her unflappable cheerfulness. On one particularly bad day on the ice, her father, faced with the daunting task of feeding so many men, addressed her in Inupiat, "Makpii, are we going to live out this year?" Her cheerful reply was, "We're living now, and we're going to keep on living!"

For those who made it to Wrangel Island, the spring and summer that followed were marked by privation and the deaths of three men. Bartlett and Kataktovik made an epic journey by sledge and foot to the Siberian mainland, then seven hundred miles along the coast of Siberia to East Cape, from where they crossed Bering Strait and reached Nome, Alaska, to arrange rescue for those stranded on the island.

The survivors of the Wrangel Island party were rescued on September 7, 1914. Despite the written record of history, family lore says that Makpii, who had turned three in April, was the first to spot the ship. "*Umiaqpak,*" she cried, as the trading vessel *King and Winge* came into view. Rescue had arrived. The following day, the twelve survivors transferred to the US Revenue steamer the *Bear*, with Bartlett aboard, and sailed for Nome. The survivors owed their lives to Bartlett and Kataktovik, and to the hunter Kurraluk and his wife. They owed nothing to Stefansson.

* * *

Makpii came through the whole terrible ordeal with only a scratch to her chin. Fred Maurer's black cat, with the tongue-twisting name of Niġigugauraq, survived the entire trip. Makpii was always chasing the cat and one day it scratched her badly, leaving a scar that was visible for the rest of her long life.

Kurraluk and his family left the ship in Nome for their long overland journey to Barrow. Makpii grew up there. Qiruk had two more children, both boys. The parents named one of them Bartlett, in honour of the fearless Newfoundland captain.

Makpii, or Ruth, as she was also known, married Fred Ipalook. They had nine children, four of whom died in infancy. Three boys and two girls grew to adulthood. A young girl was adopted in from another family. Makpii was a housewife, and later a cook in a cafeteria. She loved to sew. Emily Wilson recalled, "I learned how to sew parkas from her, and how to knit socks. Mother learned how to make dresses by looking at pictures in old catalogues." Her children taught her how to speak English as they were growing up. She was a religious woman, in a family that is still strongly Presbyterian.

The photograph of a laughing young Makpii, taken in Nome after her rescue, is the only cheerful image from an otherwise disastrous expedition.

In 2001 Makpii, then ninety years old and known as Ruth Makpii Ipalook, visited Iqaluit, Nunavut, to receive an award, presented jointly by the Canadian Polar Commission and the United States Arctic Research Commission, for her family's contribution to Arctic science. The occasion was the Arctic Science Summit, held in April of that year. Her family was belatedly being given the recognition it so richly deserved for its service to a Canadian expedition when Makpii was only an infant.

Ruth Makpii Ipalook suffered a fall and broke her hip in May of 2008. She passed away the following month in the Alaska Native Medical Center in Anchorage at the age of ninety-seven. She was buried in Utqiagvik, formerly known as Barrow.

"I Thank God for Living"

Ada Blackjack and Stefansson's Wrangel Island Fiasco

I n the summer of 2017, I was in Anchorage, Alaska, where I visited the grave of an Arctic heroine, Ada Blackjack. I found it early on a misty morning in Memorial Park Cemetery. I plucked a flower from someone else's grave—I figured they wouldn't miss it—and placed it on the rectangular plaque that marked Ada's final resting place. It was the least I could do for her.

Few people have been treated more poorly, spoken of more disparagingly, and ignored more consistently than Ada Blackjack, until recent years.

Ada was an Inuk—an Inupiaq—from Spruce Creek, Alaska, who attended a Methodist mission school in Nome when she was young. She had a son, Bennett, with her first husband, who abandoned the family.

In 1921 Ada crossed paths with the explorer Vilhjalmur Stefansson. A consummate self-promoter, Stefansson had little regard for the safety or reputations of others, and the accomplishments of his career as an Arctic explorer are marred by the list of human tragedies he left in his wake.

Stefansson had taken an interest in far-off Wrangel Island, and convinced himself that it should belong to Canada. Unfortunately, as a quick glance at a map of the Arctic regions will reveal, the island does not lie north of Canada. It does not even lie north of Alaska. Rather, it is situated directly north of Russia. But the irrepressible Stefansson insisted it must be Canadian, and sent four young men there on an expedition to raise the British flag and claim the island for Canada. Amazingly, three of the men were American. So was Ada Blackjack, twenty-three years old, who accompanied them as seamstress.

The following year, the expected supply boat did not arrive at the island. The next winter, three of the men—Allan Crawford, Fred Maurer, and Milton Galle—left for Siberia, where they hoped to secure a rescue ship. They never returned. Ada Blackjack remained on the island with Lorne Knight, who had been ill and too weak to travel.

Ada was responsible for Knight's and her own survival. She learned how to use a gun, to hunt, and to trap. But, despite Ada's efforts, Knight died of scurvy on June 22, 1923. That left Ada alone on an island teeming with polar bears.

In Those Days

In the lonely summer of 1923, Ada began using the typewriter that Milton Galle had left behind, to keep a journal. Each day before she left to hunt or scavenge for food, she would write a note on the typewriter. She was careful to always include the date, for this was more than a diary—it was a message to any rescuers who might show up during her absence, a message that she was still alive as of that morning. On July 23, the day after Knight's death, her message was brief: "I thank God for living."

In early August she finished making a boat of driftwood and canvas, the better to be able to hunt during the remainder of the summer. At the same time she finished a pair of beaded slippers for her son, although she wondered if she would ever see him again.

On the 19th of that month, rescue came in the form of a relief vessel, the *Donaldson*. The rescuers were shocked to discover that only Ada survived. Ada was equally stunned to learn that the party of three men who had left for Siberia had never reached Alaska.

Onboard the *Donaldson*, while bound for Alaska, Ada wrote out the story of her ordeal. She wrote this of her final charge, Lorne Knight: "I had hard time when he was dying. I never will forget that all my life. I was crying while he was living. I try my best to save his life but I can't quite save him."

Harold Noice, a Stefansson loyalist in charge of the rescue party, blamed Ada for Knight's death. As a result, she was vilified in the press. But Knight's parents saw the truth. They became friends with Ada. The young man's father issued a statement: "I still maintain that Ada Blackjack is a real heroine, and that there is nothing to justify me in the faintest belief that she did not do for Lorne all that she was able to do. . . . I feel that I owe [this statement] to the public and to a poor Eskimo woman who is being wronged and is helpless to defend herself."

Ada remarried and had another son, Billy Johnson, but that marriage ended in divorce. For the rest of her life, Ada battled grief, poverty, and illness. She suffered humiliation because of accusations that were occasionally made against her. She died at the age of eighty-five in Palmer, Alaska, in 1983, and was buried in Anchorage.

Billy Johnson recalled his mother this way: "I consider my mother, Ada Blackjack, to be one of the most loving mothers in this world and one of the greatest heroines in the history of Arctic exploration. She survived against all odds." Billy had a large, rectangular plaque mounted on his mother's grave. It read simply: "Heroine – Wrangel Island Expedition 1921-1923."

A month after her death, the Alaska Legislature officially recognized Ada's heroism with a citation, which it described as "a small token of remembrance for a woman whose bravery and heroic deeds have gone unnoticed for so many years."

Joe Panipakuttuk on the St. Roch

Through the Northwest Passage

I n 1944 the tiny Royal Canadian Mounted Police vessel *St. Roch* headed north from Halifax, bound for Vancouver via the Northwest Passage. En route, captain Henry Larsen stopped his vessel at Pond Inlet, the site of a police post since 1922. His purpose was to pick up an Inuit family who would provide assistance to him through the icy waters of Canada's far North.

Two years earlier, the *St. Roch* had arrived in Halifax by making the same journey, but from west to east. That journey had taken twenty-eight months, including a winter in the Arctic. On that voyage, Larsen had no Inuit assistants. But a winter in the Arctic was nothing new for the veteran captain. Norwegian born, Larsen had spent many years in the Canadian North. His vessel had been built in 1928 as a patrol and supply ship for the police and had often wintered in the Arctic. Larsen once described it as "ugly, slow and uncomfortable to live on" but with "many good qualities in a tight spot and especially in the waters she was built for."

In Halifax, the *St. Roch* had spent 1943 and early 1944 being refitted. Canada was at war, and so, when the little vessel finally left port, once again commanded by Larsen and carrying a crew of ten, her mission was shrouded in secrecy. She was to maintain Canadian sovereignty in the Arctic and to assess the feasibility of supplying far northern posts in the eastern Arctic from the west, in the event that German U-boat activity increased and became a serious threat.

On August 12 the vessel put in at Pond Inlet to pick up Joe Panipakuttuk, a hunter who had been born at Igarjuaq, a whaling and trading site just east of Pond Inlet, in 1914. He was accompanied by his wife, Letia, three children under ten years of age, and his mother, Panikpak, who went along as seamstress. Panikpak insisted on bringing her granddaughter Mary Panigusiq, whom she was raising. Joe was also accompanied by his fifteen-year-old stepson Aariak (sometimes spelled Arreak). Larsen considered Joe and Aariak to be natural-born seamen. Seventeen sled dogs were also loaded in Pond Inlet. Crew quarters were limited, and so the Inuit lived in a tent on the deck.

There have been many books and articles written about the *St. Roch*'s voyage, but it is not well known that Joe Panipakuttuk also wrote an article about his reminiscences of the trip, in Inuktitut Syllabics. It was published in *Inuktitut Magazine* in 1968, and translated and published in *north/nord* magazine the following year. He starts his memories with this:

"I remember I left Pond Inlet on the RCMP boat in the summer of 1944, on the 17th day of August. On our way we stopped at Nalluaq where I got two dogs. Captain Larsen obtained two narwhal tusks at this place. I shot one bear when we were leaving. On crossing Lancaster Sound from Nalluaq a very heavy gale set in."

They crossed the sound safely and coasted westward along the south shore of Devon Island, making a stop at the abandoned police post at Dundas Harbour. On August 20, Joe wrote, "we arrived at a small island off the west end of the big one we had been sailing alongside." They had reached Beechey Island, so well known in Qallunaat histories of the Arctic as a place where Sir John Franklin and his ill-fated crew wintered on their way into the central Arctic. But that meant little to an Inuit hunter and guide. Joe simply wrote, "It is said that in the old days some white men got lost and the head of the expedition was never found although many ships had called here searching for him. The name of the man was Franklin. On the island I saw some stone markers and graves of white men."

One of Joe's tasks was to provide fresh meat, and he was of course successful at doing so. "Two days later we left for Resolute Bay," he wrote, "and on the way I killed three walrus and a fourth at a place where the boat was touching the bottom because of the shallow water."

He recorded that Larsen and his crew erected cairns—inuksuit—at a number of places where they stopped. They went ashore on Dealy Island, a small island off Melville Island, and Joe noted the remains of a building there. "It is said that there was once a shipwreck," he wrote. "The building was made of rock with a wooden roof. They had a lot of firewood inside and quite a lot of food. The crew of this wreck had been found, it is said; they did not starve. There we found old clothing and canned food which they had left." This was the remains of a site known to history as Kellett's Storehouse, built in 1853–54 by Henry Kellett, captain of the ship *Resolute*, as a refuge and supply depot for sailors in distress. It was built of local stone, and its walls were four feet thick. When it was completed it was estimated to hold enough provisions for sixty-six men for seven months. Henry Larsen thought that nothing useful remained; it was "partially destroyed and its contents scattered everywhere by marauding bears." The shipwreck Joe referred to was probably that of the *Investigator*, farther to the west, which was abandoned in 1853 and subsequently sank.

Being from Baffin Island, Joe had never seen muskoxen before. Travelling with Larsen on Melville Island, the captain told the hunter that there were muskoxen there. "I went to where he directed me," wrote Joe, with some amusement.

> I searched the land with a telescope and saw no sign of live animals. All I could see were huge rocks. Mr. Larsen said that these were musk oxen, these very things I thought to be rocks. So I looked again through the telescope and the rocks began to move. We got near the musk oxen and I found out that they were carrying something on their backs. I thought to myself they must be carrying their little ones, but I soon learned that this was part of the animal. When you see musk oxen for the first time they have such a huge back on them![31]

Compared with the west-to-east voyage of a few years earlier, the 1944 voyage went off without a hitch. Joe guided the ship ably

---

[31] Joe Panipakuttuk, "The Reminiscences of Joe Panipakuttuk," *north/nord* (January–February 1969): 12.

through the ice, and he and Aariak hunted for fresh meat for the crew.

But Joe wasn't the only one whose knowledge of the land and sea was put to use. One crew member later remembered, "One time in the Passage we weren't sure where we were. Even Larsen was unsure. Then the Eskimo woman [Panikpak] looked at the coastline and checked with the chart. 'That's where we are,' she said. And that's where we were!"

The Inuit liked Larsen. They called him Pallursi—a word that describes someone with eyes that slope downwards at the outer corners, perhaps a sailor's squint developed from years at sea. Joe's daughter Sophie (Soopi) remembered him years later as "a straight man but a nice one," adding, "His crew was the same way because he made them that way." She remembered that the cook used to feed her and the family after the others had eaten, and that she especially liked spaghetti. But Mary Panigusiq, then aged six, disagreed: "Oh, the smell of the spaghetti that the cook would bring to my uncle at the tent. I never smelled anything so bad."

In fact, Mary would say later in life, "I hated the trip. I was very young and I was always worried. The older people didn't worry but it was terrible living in the tent on the deck. The water would come right into the tent and I got scared."

The Inuit were excited, but also a little nervous, to finally meet other Inuit when they reached Holman Island. "For the first time since leaving Pond Inlet we would now get to see a strange people and we began to feel shy," wrote Joe. Ashore, the Inuit were welcomed into the home of a man named Kanguaq. Joe noted that the settlement had only two white people, the missionary and the Hudson's Bay Company trader. "We stayed overnight there and left the following day for Tuktoyaktuk," he wrote.

About Tuktoyaktuk, he said, "That was the first time I ever heard Eskimos talk English" among themselves.

Finally the *St. Roch* reached the old whaling outpost of Herschel Island off the Yukon coast. It had been arranged that the Inuit would disembark and spend the winter there, while Larsen would take the vessel on to Vancouver. "There was a house ready for us to live in," wrote Joe. Larsen left "and we were alone there. When I looked through my binoculars and saw there was a house, some dogs and people, I became nervous. The people looked so different."

* * *

Joe spent the early fall sealing and eventually became friends with a local Inuk, who told him he was from Alaska. He took Joe with him on a caribou hunting excursion. There was a difference between the dialects spoken by the two men, but Joe said that he understood him very well. That trip broke the ice, and Joe was no longer hesitant about meeting the local people.

He and Aariak spent the winter hunting, and he recalled that "there were caribou all the time." He made a trip to Aklavik with another man, and there he encountered Indians for the first time, and more white people than he had ever seen before.

Joe was surprised at the different culture he experienced among the Inuit of the western Arctic. "The Western Inuit have ways very much like the white people and they would buy meat from me," he wrote. "I got $200 from the Inuit there just for selling them meat. When they wanted seal, they would give me $10 for it; caribou meat, $5, or if it was back meat of the caribou they would pay me $10. I told them we were all Inuit and that they should not pay me for the meat, but they said that they had to pay for everything they take from someone."

On August 11, 1945, Captain Larsen once more manoeuvred the *St. Roch* into the harbour at Herschel Island. He was surprised to find the Inuit living in a tent, because he had left them in a comfortable house the previous fall. Joe explained that there was nothing wrong with the house, but he and his family much preferred a tent in the summer. The family packed up their gear and boarded the little vessel. Their next stop was Tuktoyaktuk, where they spent two uneventful weeks before sailing on to Coppermine (now Kugluktuk), where they spent another three weeks. The passage from there to Cambridge Bay took many days. They remained there for the winter.

On April 22 of the following year, Joe and his family left Cambridge Bay, but not aboard the *St. Roch*, which Larsen had decided not to take any farther eastward. Instead they left by dog sled. Joe had eight dogs—"the same number of dogs as we had people on that journey," he wrote. Four of the eight people were young children—this would be the longest sled journey of their lives. He continued, "Our sled was twenty feet long and we had five pups besides the eight grown dogs." They were accompanied by a local guide, Kanayuk, who accompanied them as far as Gjoa Haven, where they waited for a week to replenish their supplies of dog food. There, another guide, Tiitaa, a Nattilingmiutaq, and his wife agreed to travel with them on to Ikirasak. This was Fort Ross, a Hudson's Bay Company trading post founded only in 1937 on the unofficial boundary, at least for resupply purposes, between the western and eastern Arctic.

On the way to Fort Ross, Joe took ill. Aariak and Tiitaa got a seal, but, Joe wrote, "I was so ill that I couldn't eat the meat."

They travelled on for another night—springtime travel was often at night, when the snow was firmer—and then made camp. While Aariak and Tiitaa were out in search of seal, a polar bear came into camp. Joe shot at it but missed, loosed the dogs to chase it, and eventually caught up to it and shot it where the dogs had stopped it. "I walked back feeling very sick and my lungs were sore and burning. . . . I had to stay in bed for two days feeling very weak." This was no ordinary illness. Without naming the culprit, Joe explained in his memoir, "I found out that a shaman was trying to kill me, but he killed himself instead and I got better when he died." Inuit believed that if a shaman attempted to kill another person through supernatural means and was unsuccessful because the intended victim's helping spirits were stronger than his own, that the perpetrator would die instead. This is what had happened.

They moved on and shot four caribou. By late June the snow was almost all gone from the land, and so they moved onto the sea ice. As they neared Fort Ross, they encountered a hunter, Taqulik, a man originally from Cape Dorset. When they reached the trading post, they were told that they should wait until a ship came in from the east to take them back to Pond Inlet. Joe passed the time hunting with Tiitaa and Taqulik.

Finally the famous Hudson's Bay Company ship *Nascopie* arrived, and the family was soon on the final leg of its journey home. Joe ended his narrative abruptly: "We had left Pond Inlet in 1944 and here we were coming back in 1946. It was hard for me to talk with my own people when we first got back because I kept talking in Western dialect, I had been away that long."

Joe Panipakuttuk continued to work casually for the RCMP, then signed on to the force officially in 1948 as a special constable.

In Those Days

He served for fifteen years at the force's most isolated Arctic posts: Craig Harbour, Dundas Harbour, Alexandra Fiord, Grise Fiord, and of course Pond Inlet, always with his family accompanying him. In 1951, when he moved to Craig Harbour, near present-day Grise Fiord, he was accompanied by his half-brother Kyak, another well-known special constable, and his family; they remained there for two years. Joe's stepson Aariak (Joanasie Benjamin Arreak) also became a special constable in 1948 and served for twenty years—this was indeed a police family! Joe retired to a quiet life in Pond Inlet in 1963. He died there on March 23, 1970, and is buried beneath an impressive granite headstone erected by the RCMP.

* * *

After the *St. Roch's* successful west-to-east voyage of 1940–42 through the Northwest Passage, Henry Larsen and every member of his crew had been awarded the prestigious Polar Medal. Similarly, after the completion of the single-season 1944 voyage, crew members were awarded the same medal. All except one— Joe Panipakuttuk was left out.

The Polar Medal was an evolution of the Arctic Medal, authorized by Queen Victoria in 1857, to be awarded to those who had been on expeditions of discovery or search in the Arctic between 1818 and 1855. It was later issued also to participants in the Nares expedition of 1875–76. Among the hundreds of recipients of the Arctic Medal were two Inuit, both Greenlanders: Hans Hendrik and Johan Frederick Wille, sled drivers and hunters on the Nares expedition. In 1904 the Polar Medal was created, initially to honour those who had gone to the Antarctic with the ship *Discovery* from 1902 to 1904. It was subsequently agreed that it should be awarded to participants in subsequent expeditions.

The medal is octagonal, one and a quarter inches in diameter, bearing the image of the reigning monarch on one side and, on the reverse, the ship *Discovery* in winter quarters with a sledging party in the foreground.

Joe passed away in 1970, still with no Polar Medal.

Finally, in 1974, the year that marked the thirtieth anniversary of Panipakuttuk's traverse of the passage, the error was corrected. The *St. Roch* had been decommissioned in 1954 and was declared a national historic site in 1962. In 1974, thirty years to the day after the vessel had completed its voyage to Vancouver, a ceremony was held in that city to award Joe Panipakuttuk's Polar Medal posthumously to his widow, Letia.

The issuance of Panipakuttuk's medal was rushed. The Governor General of Canada recommended the award on September 12. Canada's Solicitor General made a formal submission on September 30, noting Joe's omission from the request made for medals three decades earlier, saying that "as a result of an unfortunate oversight, the name of a Canadian Eskimo, Panipakuchoo [*sic*], was omitted from the submission at that time." The queen was asked "to approve the award of the Polar Medal to the late Panipakuchoo, who shared the hazards and difficulties of the expedition," which she did in a letter on October 8. The naval secretary requisitioned the medal two days later, and it was delivered to his office in England the following day, a Friday. The clock was ticking.

Joe's widow, Letia, arrived in Vancouver for the ceremony. She travelled from Pond Inlet with her daughter, Annie, who had also been on the voyage. Over the weekend the medal was dispatched to Ottawa, where it was received on the 15th of October. The next day, in the custody of a government official, it made it to Vancouver in the nick of time, for presentation to Letia.

Although the issuance of the medal was approved by Queen Elizabeth II, it does not bear her image on the obverse (the front). Rather, just like the medals of the crew members he travelled with in 1944, Joe's medal bears the image of the queen's father, George VI, the monarch at the time of the voyage. The clasp (the metal bar accompanying it) reads "Arctic 1944." It is, therefore, identical to the medals issued to all of Joe's adult male shipmates.

A letter from the RCMP commissioner accompanied the medal and read: "This commendation is presented to the family of the late Special Constable Panipakuchoo in recognition of his valuable contribution to the successful East-West voyage through the Northwest Passage by the Royal Canadian Mounted Police Schooner St Roch in 1944."

It went on to note that, as guide and interpreter, Panipakuttuk had "provided valuable assistance to the Captain, Sergeant H. A. Larsen, when, through his keen sense of direction and knowledge, he was able to give advice in plotting the ship's position at times when this could not be determined from the charts, and which resulted in locating the northern entrance to Prince of Wales Strait, thereby enabling the continuation and eventual completion of this historic voyage."

Joe had been a casual employee of the RCMP at the time of the voyage—he did not become a special constable until four years later. So he was not awarded the medal because of his position in the force but rather for his service to the expedition. But there were two other adults who served the expedition just as faithfully: Joe's mother, Panikpak, and his wife, Letia—not to mention Joe's stepson Aariak, who, at fifteen, worked as a hunter alongside Joe, providing food for the crew. But Joe Panipakuttuk was the only Inuk ever to be awarded the prestigious Polar Medal.

Following the death of Letia Panipakuttuk, her family donated the Polar Medal to the RCMP Museum in Regina, Saskatchewan.

Acknowledgements

All the stories contained in this volume were originally published in the author's column, Taissumani, in *Nunatsiaq News*. Original titles and publication dates are as follows:

"Abduction: The 'Countrie People' of Baffin Island Meet Martin Frobisher" originally appeared in two parts as "Abduction" on October 3, 2020, and "Five Missing Men" on October 16, 2020.

"'They Spake, But We Understood Them Not': Christopher Hall's Inuktitut Word List" originally appeared in two parts as "The First Inuktitut Word List" on August 17, 2007, and August 24, 2007.

"'Take Heed of the Savage People': Hudson's Mutineers Meet the Inuit" originally appeared in two parts as "Hudson's Mutineers and the Inuit" on January 18, 2008, and "The Knife" on January 25, 2008.

"Slaughter at Bloody Fall" originally appeared in two parts as "Slaughter at Bloody Fall" on February 6, 2021, and "Witness to

Massacre?" on February 20, 2021.

"The Return of the Dog Children: Parry and Lyon at Iglulik" originally appeared in two parts as "Parry and Lyon at Iglulik" on January 8, 2021, and "How a Stolen Shovel Led to a Shaman's Curse" on January 22, 2021.

"Parry's Medallions" originally appeared under that title on April 21, 2018.

"'A Greater Instance of Courage has not been Recorded': Tatannuaq, the Peacemaker" originally appeared as "Tatannuaq Negotiates Détente between John Franklin and the Inuit" on July 1, 2005, and incorporates excerpts from "Akaitcho and John Franklin, a Meeting of Two Chiefs" (July 28, 2006) and "The Fate of Sir John Franklin" (June 9, 2006).

"First Encounter: The Nattilingmiut Meet John Ross" originally appeared in three parts as "First Encounter: John Ross and the Nattilingmiut" on January 7, 2007, "First Encounter – The Other Side of the Story" on January 12, 2007, and "Ohokto's Story: Ross and the Nattilingmiut" on January 26, 2007.

"A Wooden Leg for Tulluahiu" originally appeared under that title on January 19, 2007.

"'The Deep Footprints of Tired Men': John Franklin's Lost Expedition" originally appeared as "The Deep Footprints of Tired Men" on May 20, 2011, and incorporates material from "The Fate of Sir John Franklin" (June 9, 2006).

"'A Nice Steady Lad and a Favourite with His Tribe': Albert One-Eye" originally appeared as "Who Was Albert One-Eye?" on June 15, 2007 and "The Fate of Albert One-Eye" on June 22, 2007, and incorporates material from "The Birth of John Rae, Arctic Explorer" (September 29, 2006).

"Charles Dickens, John Rae, and the 'Good Interpreter,' William

Ouligbuck" incorporates material from three articles: "Charles Dickens and the Inuit" (November 14, 2008), "John Rae Defends the Inuit" (November 21, 2008), and "William Ouligbuck, John Rae's Interpreter" (November 28, 2008).

"Inuit Evidence in a British Court" originally appeared in two parts under that title on February 15, 2008, and February 22, 2008.

"A Fortuitous Meeting: Tookoolito and Ipiirvik, and Charles Francis Hall" originally appeared as "A Fortuitous Meeting" on October 28, 2005, and incorporates material from "The Short Life and Sad Death of Tarralikitaq" (February 29, 2008), "Hannah and Joe on the Map" (June 27, 2008), and "Butterfly Bay" (July 4, 2008).

"Inuit Adrift: Fifteen Hundred Miles on an Ice Floe" originally appeared in two parts as "Inuit Adrift – 1500 Miles on an Ice Floe" on June 6, 2008, and "The Rescue" on June 13, 2008.

"An Inuit Plan to Find the Pole" originally appeared in three parts as "The Secret of Smith Sound" on July 16, 2010, "A School for Inuit Explorers" on July 23, 2010, and "An Inuk's Plan to Find the Pole" on July 30, 2010.

"Robert Peary, the Inughuit, and the Iron Mountain" originally appeared in four parts as "Robert Peary and the Inuit" on April 27, 2007, "The Iron Mountain" on March 21, 2008, "Peary Finds the Cape York Meteorites" on March 28, 2008, and "How to Steal a Meteorite" on April 4, 2008, and incorporates material from "Peary, the Philanthropist, Gets Paid" (April 11, 2008).

"Minik, the New York Eskimo: A Victim of Peary's Neglect" originally appeared in two parts as "Minik, the New York Eskimo – A Mock Burial" on July 20, 2018, and "Nunamingnut Uteqihut – They Have Come Home" on August 3, 2018.

"'I Will Find a Way or Fake One': Robert Peary Claims the North

Pole" incorporates material from two articles: "Robert Peary Claims the North Pole" (April 6, 2007), and "I Will Find a Way or Fake One" (April 3, 2009).

"Ittukusuk, Aapilak, and Daagtikoorsuaq: Travels with Dr. Cook" incorporates material from three articles: "Frederick Cook Claims the North Pole" (April 15, 2005), "The Race for a Telegraph Station" (April 13, 2007), and "Ittukusuk and Aapilak Islands" (October 3, 2008).

"'The Trail That Is Always New': Matthew Henson and His Inuit Family" incorporates material from two articles: "Matthew Henson, Arctic Traveller" (April 10, 2009), and "Matthew Henson: The End of the Trail That is Always New" (March 3, 2006).

"Inughuit and the Myth of Crocker Land" incorporates material from two articles: "Crocker Land, an Arctic Mirage" (April 21, 2006), and "Crocker Land, the Land that Never Was" (February 11, 2011).

"Getting Away with Murder" originally appeared under that title on April 28, 2006.

"Sovereignty 101: Captain Joseph-Elzéar Bernier and the Inuit" originally appeared in two parts as "Joseph Bernier, Canada's Polar Patriot" on July 24, 2009, and "Bernier's 1906 Expedition, Sovereignty 101 for the Inuit" on July 31, 2009, and incorporates material from "Captain Bernier and the Alienation of Inuit Land" (May 13, 2005).

"'We're Going to Keep On Living': Ruth Makpii Ipalook on Stefansson's *Karluk* Expedition" incorporates material from two articles: "The Sinking of the *Karluk*" (January 6, 2006), and "Ruth Makpii Ipalook – 1911–2008" (July 18, 2008).

"'I Thank God for Living': Ada Blackjack and Stefansson's

In Those Days

Wrangel Island Fiasco" originally appeared as "The Grave of Ada Blackjack, Heroine" on March 24, 2018, and incorporates material from "The Death of Ada Blackjack" (May 26, 2006).

"Joe Panipakuttuk on the *St. Roch:* Through the Northwest Passage" originally appeared in three parts as "Joe Panipakuttuk on the St. Roch: Through the Northwest Passage" on August 7, 2020, "Joe Panipakuttuk on the St. Roch: Winter at Herschel Island and Getting Home" on August 21, 2020, and "Joe Panipakuttuk's Polar Medal" on September 4, 2020.